Antisocial Personality Disorder and Criminal Justice

Evidence-Based Practices for Offenders & Substance Abusers

Dr. Gregory L. Little
Dr. Kenneth D. Robinson
Katherine D. Burnette, M.S.
E. Stephen Swan, M.Ed.

Eagle Wing Books, Inc.
Memphis, Tennessee

Antisocial Personality Disorder and Criminal Justice: Evidence-Based Practices for Offenders & Substance Abusers

Published by
Eagle Wing Books, Inc.
P.O. Box 9972
Memphis, TN 38190

www.moral-reconation-therapy.com
www.ccimrt.com

ISBN 10: 0940829401
ISBN 13: 9780940829404

Retail Price: $18.95

Table of Contents

Chapter 1

Introduction

There is a purpose to psychiatric diagnosis. It is to enable mental
health professionals to...communicate with each other..., comprehend
the pathological processes..., and control psychiatric outcomes.
Robert Spitzer *DSM — III* (1975)

The need for a classification of mental disorders has been clear
throughout the history of medicine... *DSM — IV* (1994)

The practical fields of criminology, criminal justice, drug abuse,
and others that deal directly with behavioral disorders have not
traditionally incorporated biological or genetic perspectives.
Fishbein *The Science, Treatment & Prevention of Antisocial Behaviors* (2000)

The field of criminal justice has a nearly endless list of important and
enduring questions and this book seeks to provide some basic answers
to them. What causes crime? How many criminals are in America?
What is the relationship between drugs and crime? Can anyone become an addict? Can anyone become a criminal? Is there such a thing
as a criminal personality? If so, what causes a criminal personality?
Can we reduce the crime rate? Can we build enough prisons and jail
cells to incarcerate all the criminals? How many prisoners actually come
back to prison after they serve their sentences and are released to the
community? Are there certain types of prisoners who are more likely to
return to prison? Can we really rehabilitate criminals? If so, what types
of programs are actually effective rehabilitation strategies? Are some
treatment programs so ineffective that they are a waste of money? Do
some treatment programs actually increase offending? Can medications
reduce criminality? Is the actual incarceration of most criminals even
necessary? Can we reliably predict which criminals can be rehabili-
tated? Can we reliably predict whether a particular criminal will recidivate? Can we predict future violence? Are all criminals the same? Is
criminality genetic, learned, or both? Is it caused by societal condi-

tions? There are a lot more questions that could be listed here but these are a good start.

In this book there are statistics, debate points made on different sides of each question, and summaries of outcome results from vast areas of research encompassing the entire field. The book focuses on one very important and consistent finding: **The majority of individuals who are deemed criminals by the criminal justice system are diagnosable with a psychological disorder classified as a *Personality Disorder*.** The specific disorder is termed *Antisocial Personality Disorder* **(ASPD)**, and it has traditionally been considered to be almost untreatable with the only significant progress in its treatment seen in the past 20 years. In addition, the vast majority of offenders are also substance abusers, and this fact has greatly confounded our understanding of the nature of criminality and what sort of treatment strategies are best applied—if any. The focus of this book is on the incidence, characteristics, implications, and treatment of Antisocial Personality Disorder, which is prevalent in criminal justice populations.

Personality Disorders & Criminality

Personality disorders have long been described by psychology and psychiatry as an enduring set of characteristics, traits, and behaviors. Personality disorders are not a psychosis and really can't be described as mental illness in the usual sense of the term. Nor can they be described as *insane*, which is a legal term that generally implies not knowing the difference between right and wrong. The easiest way to comprehend a person with ASPD is to understand that he or she knows the difference between right and wrong, but the person just doesn't care. They have a type of psychological and psychiatric *disorder* with profound implications. This will be explained in some detail in later sections. In essence, the relationship of criminality to personality disorders implies that criminality (meaning the propensity to engage in criminal behavior) lies *within* the individual. From this perspective, crime is a consequence of how one views the world and others, what the person believes about the world and others, and what behaviors are acceptable to the individual. However, it should be understood that the idea that *criminality lies within the individual* does **not** mean that there are not a host of causes. In brief, ASPD is something we can describe as a criminal personality but it has many variations. Not all of these variations can be described as criminal.

Complicating this view is the fact that some professionals point to society as the culprit in producing crime and Antisocial Personality. They assert that poverty, racism, lack of education, lack of job skills or opportunity, poor parenting, childhood abuse, sexual abuse, and media factors all contribute to crime—or actually *cause* it. In truth, the wide-ranging field of criminal justice is enmeshed in a swirling set of often ill-defined and misunderstood issues and causal factors. These factors intertwine and interact to create a confusing set of vastly opposing theories and simplistic solutions that can sometimes cause more harm than good. An important thing to keep in mind regarding the debate between society being the cause of crime as opposed to crime being an individual's choice is the day-to-day reality of people who work in the system. That reality is this: we have individuals entering the system who have to be managed, supervised, and hopefully helped. These individuals are, at least to some extent, a product of society. But it's not society that the criminal justice system copes with every day. We can't treat society in prison or in supervision programs. We can only treat the individuals in the system, and in so doing, hopefully, we can affect society in a beneficial way.

Nothing in this discussion suggests that poverty, racism, increasing violence depicted in the media, sex abuse, childhood abuse, poor parenting, education, and many other issues don't relate or contribute to criminality. In truth, all of these issues are clearly related to various types of crime, drug abuse, and other problems. It's just that professionals working with individuals and groups of offenders who are in the system have very real limits on what they can do about these societal issues. Acknowledging that such issues do play a role in criminality is one thing, but utilizing the information in a beneficial way is another.

While this book is primarily about Antisocial Personality Disorder and its treatment, an overview of the entire field of criminal justice in America is necessary. And it is here where we begin.

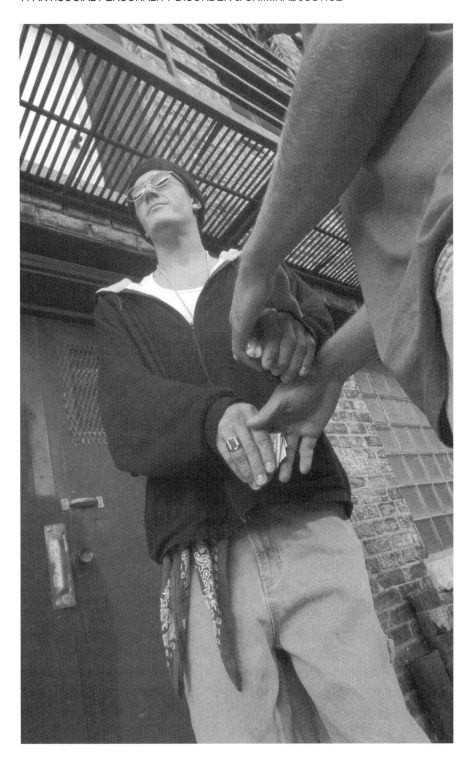

Chapter 2

The Numbers—The Extent of Criminal Justice in America

Criminal justice in America is an enormous industry. It includes police and related enforcement agencies, courts at all governmental levels, probation and parole, jails, prisons, the ever-expanding private corrections business, offender treatment and programs located in virtually every level of society, and a wide range of support and product supply industries. Materials consumed include enormously expensive concrete and steel prisons, razor wire and fencing, steel bars, clothing and bedding, electronics and locks, extensive computer systems, cell and agency phones, paper and pens, copy machines, automobiles, guns, protection equipment, and so much more covering virtually every conceivable consumer product. Prisons could be considered to be the most expensive, comprehensive housing and self-enclosed "support system" in America. Although estimates of the total expenditures made in criminal justice efforts vary widely, the National Institute of Justice (Anderson, 1999) calculates that 49 million crimes occur in America each year with the total cost over $1 trillion. Over a decade ago, the annual cost of America's corrections operations alone was $400 billion. The cost of corrections, associated crime costs, and all security measures in America itself accounted for over $1 trillion.

The cost of corrections, associated crime costs, and all security measures in America accounts to over $1 trillion a year.

Over 14 million people move through the quickly revolving doors of the American criminal justice system each year, with a substantial number of these people moving back and forth several times a year. It is a massive and intricate patchwork machine of interdependent agencies that often operates smoothly but sometimes becomes clogged by overwhelming numbers. It is largely driven by two related human issues: substance use and abuse, and individuals afflicted with personality disorders.

Arrests In America & Adult System Capacity

The total number of arrests made for criminal infractions in America each year—excluding all simple non-DUI traffic violations—now averages 14.3 million (FBI, Uniform Crime Reports, 2008). About 13 percent of all arrests are directly related to drug law violations (not including those who are drug abusers performing other crimes to support their habit). In mid-2008, American jails; Federal, state, and county prisons; and private correctional facilities held 2.4 million adult individuals in custody (Bureau of Justice Statistics, 2009). Private correctional facilities housed 126,000 of these individuals. While there is great variability depending on the specific location, American jails operate on an average at 95 percent of capacity, housing nearly 786,000 individuals. In recent years, jail capacity has increased about 2 percent annually due to new construction, and in 2012 about 900,000 people will be in jails. Of the 14.3 million arrests cited in the first sentence of this paragraph, 13.6 million people actually enter and are subsequently processed in a jail. Obviously, since jails hold less than 1 million people, the vast majority of these 13.6 million are quickly released pending their case disposition. Jails are literally a revolving door where people quickly move in and out. With a capacity of less than 1 million, it should be obvious that jails are intended to be a revolving door—a fast processing short-term holding facility. Because of this, the bond industry is one of the largest private sector businesses in criminal justice.

American prisons house 1.5 million individuals serving sentences ranging from a few months to life. Although these numbers vary drastically by state, America's prisons are operating on average 8 percent above their rated capacity. The Federal system is operating at higher

America's Criminal Justice System

How the system handles more than 14 million arrests each year.

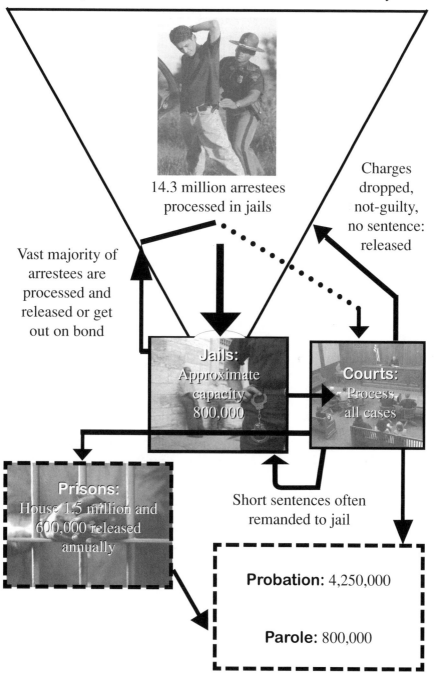

14.3 million arrestees processed in jails

Charges dropped, not-guilty, no sentence: released

Vast majority of arrestees are processed and released or get out on bond

Jails: Approximate capacity 800,000

Courts: Process all cases

Prisons: House 1.5 million and 600,000 released annually

Short sentences often remanded to jail

Probation: 4,250,000

Parole: 800,000

levels above rated capacity, but private correctional facilities can and have quickly added bed space. The huge costs of building, maintaining, and managing prisons has made prisons a key political issue for taxpayers. Over 600,000 prisoners are released each year from America's prisons (Petersilia, 2004) meaning that 4 out of every 10 prisoners are released each year.

One frequently asked question posed at the beginning of this book is, "Can we build our way out of the crisis?" The answer is, of course, **yes**. We *could* construct more prisons and jails—a lot more—and do so quickly. We would just need to find the will and come up with the money—or simply print the money—an issue beyond the scope of this book. The more relevant question is *should* we build more prisons and jails? Do we already have sufficient capacity? Are there other things we can do to reduce the need for prisons and jails? Those questions are within the scope of this book and will be addressed.

Adult Offenders Under
Federal, State, & Local Jurisdictions

The Bureau of Justice Statistics (BJS) and other Federal agencies routinely issue reports on inmate populations as well as the number of offenders under some sort of probation and parole (Bureau of Justice Statistics, 1992a, b). These numbers include only adults over the age of 18 (with very few exceptions). Thus, juveniles under supervision are discussed in a later section of this chapter.

Incarceration and criminal justice supervision rates are often officially issued as a number per 100,000 people of the population, which is a continuation of a custom that was adapted from epidemiological reporting of disease rates. When the numbers per 100,000 were

Of the entire population of United States adults, 3.2 percent are under some form of criminal justice supervision— in jail or prison — or on parole or probation.

relatively low, this epidemiological system made sense especially when the resulting percentage was well below one percent. However, with the increases in criminal populations in the modern era, the epidemiological reporting method could be seen as outdated and confusing. For the purposes of simplicity, this text has converted the rate per 100,000 to the actual percentage of the *adult* population. In brief, 3.2 percent of the *adult* population in the US is under some level of criminal justice supervision. As can be seen in the more detailed discussion below, this percentage has increased over the past few decades.

U.S. Census reports reveal that adults 18 years and older have consistently comprised about 75% of the total U.S. population. The annual U.S. Bureau of Census statistics were utilized to gather the relevant population figures for each year reported below. A simple summary statement of these data is as follows.

From 1990 to 2007, the percentage of all American adults under some form of criminal justice supervision went from 2.3 percent to 3.2 percent. This increase (nine tenth of one percent) may seem trivial, but is actually almost a 40 percent increase (.9 / 2.3 = .391). In the foreseeable future it is expected that this percentage will remain stable. The following section details these figures.

From 1990 to 2008

In 1990, BJS reported that 4.3 million adults were under some sort of criminal justice supervision in the United States. That figure represented about 2.3% of the total adult population at that time. More than half (61%) of these offenders were on probation while another 12% were on parole. About 17% were in prison while the remainder (9%) were in a jail. Thus, in 1990, only 26% of convicted (or current) offenders were incarcerated.

In 1994, 5.1 million adults were under criminal justice supervision representing 2.7% of the adult population. Probation (58%) and parole (13.5%) accounted for the majority of offenders while 19% were in prison and 9.5% were in a jail. In 1994, about 28.5% of convicted (or current) offenders were incarcerated.

In 2000, 6.4 million adults were under criminal justice supervision representing 3.05% of the total adult population. Most of these were on probation (59%) and parole (11%). Prisons (20%) and jails (10%) incarcerated the remainder. In 2000, about 30% of convicted (or current) offenders were incarcerated.

In 2005, 6.9 million adults were under criminal justice supervision representing 3.1% of the total adult population. About 30% were in prison or jails while 59% were on probation and 9% were on parole (Hora & Stalcup, 2008).

At the beginning of 2007, 7.2 million adults were under criminal justice supervision representing 3.2% of the total adult population. The majority of these were on probation (59%) and parole (11%) while jails (10%) and prisons (20%) incarcerated the remainder (Bureau of Justice Statistics, 2009).

Summary. The vast majority of offenders who are actively supervised by some level of criminal justice (about 70%) are not incarcerated. These individuals are on some level of probation or parole supervision. The remainder of offenders (about 30%) are incarcerated at the Federal, state, or local level. Over the past 15 years, the percentage of all offenders who are on probation and parole has remained remarkably consistent, as has the percentage of incarcerated offenders. In essence, the relative percentage of offenders who are incarcerated has remained consistent, although, as indicated above, the actual numbers have increased (as the overall population increased), leading to a large expansion in prison and jail space.

On the other hand, during the 1990s the percentage of the total American adult population under *any type* of criminal justice supervision increased. In 1990, this percentage was 2.3, by 1994 it was 2.7, and by 2000 the percentage was 3.05. In 2005 the percentage of adults under criminal justice supervision was 3.1 and in 2007 the figure stood at 3.2%. (*Figures 1 and 2* depict the key issues cited here.)

In 2007, 7.2 million adults were under some form of criminal justice supervision in the United States.

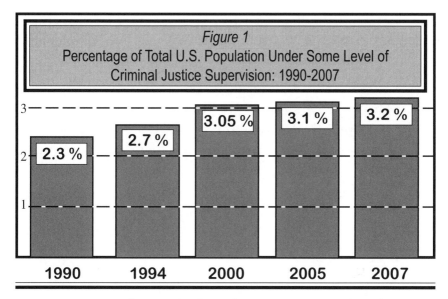

Figure 1
Percentage of Total U.S. Population Under Some Level of
Criminal Justice Supervision: 1990-2007

In essence, from 1990 (2.3%) to 2007 (3.2%), the relative percentage of offenders in the entire criminal justice system (as a percentage of total adult population) increased by 39.1%. [Here is the calculation: 3.2 - 2.3 = .9; .9 / 2.3 = .391]. In "human" terms, there were 2.9 million more individuals in the criminal justice system in 2007 as compared to 1990. However, the U.S. population increased by 59 million people during the same period. From 2007 to early 2009, the population increased by another 4 million people. Thus, in 2009, it is reliably

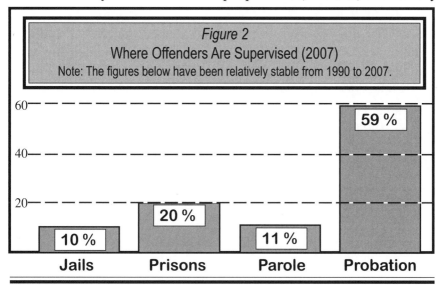

Figure 2
Where Offenders Are Supervised (2007)
Note: The figures below have been relatively stable from 1990 to 2007.

estimated that 7.3 million adults were under some level of criminal justice supervision. In 2010 the number will be 7.4 or 7.5 million. The numbers should rise proportionally over subsequent years as the population increases.

The U.S. Incarceration Rate—Currently the Highest in the World—One in 100 Adults: Rates For Minority Groups are Significantly Higher

The term *incarcerate* is derived from the combination of two Latin words: *in* + *carcer* (prison). It simply means to put in prison or to place someone in confinement. Some time ago before its collapse, the former Soviet Union and a few other countries had higher incarceration rates than the United States. As mentioned earlier, incarceration rates are typically given in epidemiological terms, the number per 100,000 of population. A simple comparison of incarceration rates between different countries is complicated and does not give a completely accurate picture. This is because children and adolescents are not typically confined but are often included in the rate per 100,000 population. Different countries can and do have vastly different proportions of people under the age of 18; thus, meaningful comparisons are not as simple as comparing the rates of incarceration as usually cited. However, there is little doubt among anyone in the field that in the developed world, the U.S. has the highest incarceration rate.

The Hoover Institution (2008) issued a comparison of different countries' incarceration rates based on the most available data, which was collected at the end of 2006. The U.S. led the world with a rate of 751 people per 100,000. Russia was second with 628. Within the U.S., Louisiana had the highest rate of all states with 835 people incarcerated per 100,000. Maine had the lowest rate with about 148 per 100,000.

When only the adult population is used to calculate the U.S. incarceration rate, the result is easy to understand and remember. The Pew Center (Warren, *et al.*, 2008) issued a large report on the actual incarceration rate of all 50 states and the U.S. based strictly on the adult population (over age 18). The title of the report gave the overall result: *One In 100: Behind Bars in America 2008*. They found that about one individual for every 100 adults in America is currently incar-

Quick Facts—

• About 3.2% of the U.S. adult population is on some sort of criminal justice supervision at any given time.

• From 1990 to the present, the percentage of the U.S adult population who are involved in the criminal justice system has increased from 2.3 to 3.2 percent. However the largest increase was between 1990 to 2000. Since 2000 the increase has been slight.

• The majority (70%) of all offenders who are on criminal justice supervision are not incarcerated. They are on probation or parole.

• About 20% of offenders are incarcerated in prisons.

• About 10% of offenders are in local jails.

• One in every 100 American adults is incarcerated.

cerated in a prison or jail. The rates of incarceration for different racial and ethnic categories revealed a wide disparity that has long been obvious to everyone working in the criminal justice system.

Who Is Incarcerated

Jails in America are typically used for brief processing or temporary imprisonment. Arrestees who are awaiting bond or trial appearances, those serving brief sentences for DUI or simple misdemeanors, and those convicted with sentences under a year comprise the bulk of people housed in jails. The U.S. incarceration rate includes those housed in jails as well as prisons, where inmates are typically serving sentences for more than a year. Of the 2.4 million people incarcerated in prisons and jails, about 93% are male and 7% are female.

Males Incarcerated by Race/Ethnicity. About 93% of the 2.4 million people who are incarcerated are male. Of America's total population of adult white males, one in every 106 is incarcerated. One in every 36 adult Latino males is incarcerated. One in every 15 adult black males is incarcerated. The proportion of incarcerated Latino and black males is significantly higher than that of white males.

Females Incarcerated by Race/Ethnicity. About 7% of the 2.4 million people who are incarcerated are female. Of America's total population of adult white females, one in every 859 is incarcerated. One in every 436 adult Latino females is incarcerated and one in every 203 adult black females is incarcerated. The proportion of incarcerated Latino and black females is significantly higher than that of white females.

Why The Racial Disparity? Clearly, the disproportionate number of minorities within criminal justice is a major and important societal issue. As will be presented in later chapters, research shows that it is not due to higher incidences of ASPD or psychopathy in minority groups, nor do any of the genetic, physiological, or hormonal studies point out differences between minority groups and others. Kappeler, Blumberg, & Potter (2000) relate, "The drug war, particularly intensive street-level drug enforcement, has been blatantly racist." According to research cited in the Kappler, *et al.* textbook, blacks comprise 11% of America's drug users but account for 37% of all drug arrests. Other research shows that "blacks are far more likely to get prison sentences for drug law violations. Overall, 54% of African Americans get sentenced to prison as opposed to 34% of whites for the same drug offenses. In drug possession cases, 44% of blacks get prison time as compared to 29% of whites, and in trafficking cases 60% of blacks go to prison as opposed to 37% of whites." Few people will dispute the statistics but the issue can be interpreted several ways. However, the majority of criminal justice professionals accept that race, poverty, education, and access to various resources all play a role in the overrepresentation of minorities in criminal justice.

Juvenile Justice

Reliable and accurate statistics on the number of juvenile offenders in America are not available or are perhaps sometimes concealed for a host of possible reasons. The Office of Juvenile Justice and Delinquency Prevention (OJJDP) relates that there are no reliable figures on how many juvenile cases actually occur each year because many cases are handled informally, sometimes only with family involvement, and often without any processed paperwork. Note that this is not a criticism, simply an acknowledgement that juvenile justice is typically operated quite differently than the adult system. The OJJDP (Delinquency Cases in Juvenile Court, 2005—published in 2009) estimates that approximately 1.7 million formal cases are handled annually, but that estimate is probably too low and does not reflect the informal cases. Females comprise 27 percent of the total juveniles who are processed, with whites (64%) and blacks (33%) representing the bulk of cases. In 21 percent of all cases, the juvenile is detained until a formal court proceeding. Less than one-half of one percent of all juvenile cases are moved to adult courts. In 60 percent of all juvenile cases, some form of probation was ordered. It is interesting to note that although ASPD behavior is observed in juveniles, there are limited interventions available to probation to correct this challenge.

Quick Facts—

• About 93 percent of incarcerated offenders are male.

• Black and Latino inmates comprise a statistically disproportionate share of incarcerated offenders.

• Less than 1 percent of juvenile cases go to adult courts.

Chapter 3

Recidivism in Offender Populations

The term *recidivism* comes from the Latin word *recidivus*. The Latin word means "recurring" or "falling back" and implies that a person repeats an undesirable behavior after being previously treated or punished for performing the behavior. With offenders, the term typically means offenders who are either rearrested or actually return to prison. Thus, one thing that should always be noted is the precise definition used for recidivism when such statistics are encountered—it could mean rearrests (either any arrests or only arrests for certain types of crime), reincarceration, or any variation or combination of these. When an offender is rearrested, that offender is in reality a recidivist. A recidivism rate is the percentage of offenders who are rearrested or return to prison after a given period of time. Many in the criminal justice field, including the present authors, believe that a reduction in recidivism should be the overriding goal in criminal justice—assuming that public safety is the main concern—but recidivism should be the primary guiding principle in the application of most programs to offender groups.

"What's your recidivism rate?"

That question is frequently asked of programs and agencies dealing with offenders. The answer is not always as easy to explain as it might seem. One very important issue involved is that a program, institution, or agency's recidivism rate depends on how long its clients have been released. A one-year recidivism rate is lower than a two-year rate, which is lower than a three-year rate, and so on. In short, the more time an offender has been released, the greater the opportunity for rearrest and reincarceration. While there are notable exceptions to this, most programs utilize very brief time periods in analyzing recidivism and few exceed 3 years. Many programs cite exceptionally low recidivism rates but fail to state that they have collected such data for three months or often less. Individual states compile recidivism statistics that are often vastly different in the criteria employed to define recidivism. Many states only count felony rearrests or actual arrests with a conviction and new sentence. Most states only count rearrests in their particular state and recidivism within their own prisons. In that case, a violent offender who moves to another state and is convicted of murder isn't a recidivist—that offender is counted as a success in that state's recidivism statistic. Such details are often buried somewhere within reports or are simply not related at all. Recidivism reports that do not give a precise definition and a timeframe should be viewed with skepticism.

Most states routinely publish some sort of recidivism data and make it available to the public on websites. Those who search such information should carefully examine the definition of recidivism in any particular study as well as the timeframe studied. The U.S. Bureau of Justice Statistics has conducted several large studies of prisoner recidivism as well as parole and probation recidivism. More recidivism research will be presented in the chapter on treatment approaches applied to offenders, but the basic overall numbers are found below.

Prison recidivism. In June 2002 the Bureau of Justice Statistics released a study of over 272,000 offenders released from prisons in 15 states. The study began in 1994 and tracked the three-year recidivism rate analyzing three types of recidivism: rearrests, reconvictions, and reincarceration. Results showed that within the three years after their release, 67.5 percent of all released prisoners had been rearrested. Within the three years, 46.9 percent had been reconvicted and 51.8 percent had been reincarcerated. The reincarceration rate (51.8) being higher than the reconviction rate (46.9) is due to the fact that some prisoners were returned to prison for what are called technical violations.

Jail recidivism. Relatively little data has been published on jail inmate recidivism; however, the research that exists has results similar to that found in prisons. For example, Krueger (1997) evaluated the rearrest rates of over 7,000 inmates released from an Ohio jail. Within one year after processing and release, 51 percent had been rearrested for some offense. A sample of these jail inmates who had been released for 5 years showed that 95 percent had been rearrested.

Parole recidivism. A 2006 study published in the Journal of the American Probation and Parole Association (Solomon, 2006) utilized statistics from the 2002 Bureau of Justice data mentioned in the prior paragraph. The study evaluated the three-year recidivism of 38,624 parolees who were released from prison starting in 1994. The report showed that 59 percent of all parolees were rearrested within three years.

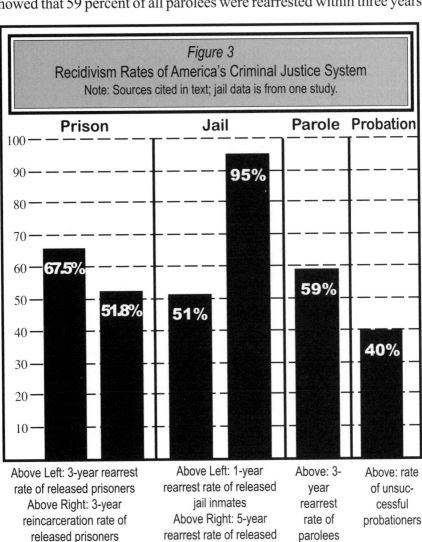

Figure 3
Recidivism Rates of America's Criminal Justice System
Note: Sources cited in text; jail data is from one study.

| Above Left: 3-year rearrest rate of released prisoners
Above Right: 3-year reincarceration rate of released prisoners | Above Left: 1-year rearrest rate of released jail inmates
Above Right: 5-year rearrest rate of released jail inmates | Above: 3-year rearrest rate of parolees | Above: rate of unsuccessful probationers |

The study concluded, "Parole has not contributed substantially to reduced recidivism and increased public safety."

Probation recidivism. In 2004, the Bureau of Justice Statistics published a large report on probation in America. According to that study, in 2004 over 6 million individuals served a probation term, many of which were relatively brief. Just over half of these were serving a sentence for a misdemeanor. Drug law violators (26%) and DWI (15%) were the two largest categories of probationers. A substantial percentage of probationers (26%) have no reporting requirements whatsoever; these individuals are simply considered to be successful if they don't get rearrested. Probation recidivism is often defined in terms of those who do not successfully complete their probation. Results showed that 40 percent of probationers are not successful; however, the 9 percent that had absconded are neither counted as failures nor successes—unless their probation term expired before they were found.

Juvenile Offenders & Recidivism

One of the most difficult statistics to ascertain in the entire field of criminal justice is recidivism of juvenile offenders. The Office of Juvenile Justice and Delinquency Prevention (OJJDP) relates that no national recidivism statistics exist on juveniles because states and local jurisdictions report such figures in vastly different ways, collect information in different manners (if at all), and do not handle juvenile cases similarly. Literally hundreds of small sample recidivism reports have been published on juvenile offenders with many comparing various treatment approaches to some form of control or comparison groups. These studies cannot be used for evaluating statewide systems for the simple reason that such research used differing definitions of recidivism and studied highly specialized samples of offenders such as sex offenders, violent juveniles, and specific types of substance abusers. The variability and inconsistent definitions in juvenile recidivism research is exemplified by two published state reports evaluating relatively large populations. In 2008 the Indiana Department of Correction (Indiana, 2008) evaluated the recidivism of 1,493 juveniles for the three years after their date of "release" from some form of detention. Their definition of recidivism was "a return to reincarceration within three years" (either to juvenile or adult facilities). Using that criterion they found that *only* 35.9 percent of juveniles were "recidivists." By contrast, in 2005 Washington State (State of Washington, 2005) evaluated the recidivism of 13,127 juveniles who had received a "disposition" in that year. Their definition of recidivism was "any disposition in which the offender's juvenile history contains a disposition." There was no length of time included in the definition of recidivism, which means their definition of recidivism was: the percentage of juveniles who entered the system in 2005 who had previously entered the system on some other "charge." That is, the study answered the question: How many of 13,127 juveniles who had dispositions in 2005 had at least one earlier disposition? They found that 76 percent of juveniles were prior offenders—or recidivists. MacKenzie's (2006) groundbreaking book, *What Works in Corrections*, contains a chapter on juvenile recidivism. While the chapter focuses on the comparison of recidivism of untreated juveniles to groups of offenders treated with various strategies, nearly all of the dozens of studies showed recidivism results in the range of the two large reports cited above.

Quick Facts—

• More than half of incarcerated offenders will return to prison within three years after release.

• Nearly 60 percent of parolees will be rearrested within three years of parole initiation.

• Forty percent of probationers fail to successfully complete probation and another 9 percent abscond.

• About 75 percent of juvenile offenders are recidivists and about 36 percent will return to incarceration within three years.

Chapter 4

Incarceration & Drug Use

A relationship between substance use/abuse and incarceration is well established and accepted as factual (Little & Robinson, 1997). In brief, crime, incarceration, and substance abuse are clearly linked together. Research from a variety of sources has consistently shown that the vast majority of offenders routinely use drugs and/or alcohol. These estimates range between 70 to 100 percent (Little & Robinson, 1997) depending on the type of offense. This relationship is often *interpreted* as causal in that it is implied that substance use or abuse causes criminality. Several secondary substance use relationships found with criminality are typically mentioned to strengthen the implied causality between using drugs and criminal behavior. These relationships are described below; however, it should be noted, "correlation is not causation." What this often-stated statistical caution shows is that because a large proportion of offenders self-report drug use, drug abuse, and addiction; it does not mean that drug use causes crime, nor that crime causes drug use. This issue will be addressed again in later sections.

Data on offender drug use comes from various sources; however, the statistics cited by particular institutions and organizations sometimes depends on the focus, purpose, or agenda of the reporting agency. Self-reports from offenders are typically utilized because they cost little and are easy to obtain. Self-reports, where the offender simply answers questions about the drugs used, are not as accurate as chemical tests of hair or urine screens. They rely on honesty and some self-awareness. Despite their obvious limitations, self-reports do serve a purpose and they are the standard nearly always utilized to make diagnoses.

Offenders' self-reported drug use. Literally hundreds of studies have confirmed that offenders tend to report drug use at levels far exceeding the non-offender population's reported levels. Depending on the type of offense category studied, somewhere between 70 to 100 percent of offenders either self-report drug use or are found to be drug users. In some studies, the drug usage has actually been confirmed through drug tests analyzing urine, saliva, or hair. A 1998 Bureau of Justice Statistics survey reported that 70 percent of probationers reported drug use. A 2005 report (BJS) showed that 68 percent of jail inmates were drug dependent or drug abusers. A 2006 report (BJS) revealed that 83 percent of Federal and state prisoners reported drug use. A 2007 report (NCJRS, 2007) found that the levels of reported drug usage by arrestees remains stable.

Self-reported crime to obtain money for drugs. The Bureau of Justice Statistics (2005; 2006) reports that 17.5 percent of all prisoners (state and Federal) related that they committed their current offense to obtain money for drugs. Within local jails, about 25 percent of property and drug offenders self-reported that they committed their current offense to obtain money for drugs. It is not known if these figures genuinely reflect the actual situation; however, it is highly likely that they do.

Self-reported drug use at the time of crime. In 1998 the Bureau of Justice Statistics released the first national survey of probationers who admitted to being under the influence of drugs at the time of their current crime. The survey showed that 14 percent of state probationers self-reported that they were under the influence of drugs when they committed their current offense. A 2006 report by the Bureau of Justice Statistics found that 32 percent of state prisoners and 26 percent of Federal prisoners self-reported that they were under the influence of drugs when they committed their current offense. However, that same report revealed that 74 percent of prisoners with mental health problems were dependent (addicted) to drugs or alcohol while 56 percent of prisoners without a mental health diagnosis showed dependence. Jail populations showed essentially the same results. Those convicted of robbery, weapons violations, burglary, and motor vehicle theft were the most likely to report drug dependence and abuse.

Quick Facts—

• The vast majority of offenders (68 to 100 percent) at all levels of criminal justice self-report drug use.

• About 17.5 percent of all offenders report they committed their current offense to obtain money for drugs.

• Only 14 percent of probationers, 26 percent of Federal prisoners, and 32 percent of state prisoners reported they were under the influence of drugs at the time of their actual crime.

• Inmates with mental health problems show the highest rate (74 percent) of self-reported drug dependence.

Chemical Testing of Offenders
For Drug Usage Yields Different Results

With the advent of drug testing utilizing urinalysis and hair analysis, the extent of substance abuse in offenders is becoming more apparent. The incidence of substance abuse among arrestees is astonishing. "Some voluntary surveys have shown that about 35% of inmates admit to being under the influence of drugs at the time of their offense... [but] drug testing of arrestees has shown that the vast majority of those charged for crimes were positive for drugs at the time of their arrest" (Bureau of Justice Statistics, 1992a; b—cited in Little & Robinson, 1994; *emphasis added*). Specifically, the 1992 Bureau of Justice urine drug-testing program on arrestees (with samples taken at the time of the arrest) showed that **up to 75% had cocaine in their** systems at the time of their arrest. **Nearly 90% were under the influence of either drugs or alcohol when arrested.** Similar high drug usage rates among arrestees have continued to be reported by the Bureau of Justice. Hemphill, Hart, and Hare (1994) reported that 96% of Canadian inmates diagnosed as psychopaths (a controversial description of ASPD) using the Hare Psychopathy Checklist had substance abuse disorders (and 89% of the remaining inmates also showed substance abuse problems).

From the above research it is clear that voluntary drug or alcohol usage surveys of offenders may grossly underestimate the actual incidence of drug usage. The simplest explanation is that when asked about their drug use, offenders are trying to minimize the extent of their drug problems. For example, a study of 165 consecutive juvenile arrestees in Cleveland, Ohio showed how unreliable voluntary drug usage information from juveniles is when it is collected through intake questionnaires (Freucht, Stephens, & Walker, 1994). In that study only 7.4% of all juvenile arrestees admitted to *ever* using cocaine. Urinalysis testing indicated that 8% had cocaine metabolites in their bodies *at the time of their arrest*. However, the Cleveland study also performed hair analysis, the most accurate of all current drug usage testing methods. Results showed that *60% of the arrestees had used cocaine within the last 30 days.* Thus, the voluntary drug usage information was fully eight times less than actual use when the testing information was analyzed for only the past 30 days. Magura, Kang, and Shapiro (1995) reported on a near replication of the Cleveland study with older offenders. Their study "recruited" 121 male arrestees (mean age 19 years) and found that 36% admitted to using cocaine at least once in their lives. Hair analysis showed that 67% had used cocaine in the last 30 days. This research shows that the validity of self-reports is questionable at best, and completely misleading at worst. In short, arrestees tend to minimize their drug usage.

Research shows that up to 90 percent of arrestees might be under the influence of drugs or alcohol at the time of their arrest.

Perhaps the most reliable survey of offender drug use comes from the Arrestee Drug Abuse Monitoring (ADAM) program, which monitors drug use in 39 municipal areas through drug urine testing. In 2003, ADAM found that 73.6 percent of female arrestees and 73.9 percent of male arrestees had metabolites of at least one of nine drugs or alcohol in their bodies within 48 hours of their arrest. The 2007 results were very similar (Zhang, 2003; 2007).

Quick Facts—

• Self-reported drug use by offender populations appears to underreport the actual level and extent of drug usage. Juveniles tend to underreport to a larger extent than do adult offenders.

• The implications of these findings remain unclear. It may well be that such findings change rapidly and are dependent on the type of drug usage and type of crime. Most of the research has focused on cocaine usage. It is possible that self-reports on the use of heroin, methamphetamine, marijuana, and other drugs may be more accurate.

Chapter 5

Antisocial Personality Disorder & The DSM Axes

One of the most problematic and misunderstood issues in treating substance abusers and offender populations is the remarkably large proportion of people in these groups who have a coexisting Personality Disorder (PD). This fact has been greatly misunderstood or discounted by many in the criminal justice field. Treatments for PDs have always been viewed as rather ineffective, and when a PD co-exists with a substance abuse problem, treatment effectiveness becomes even more tenuous (Fishbein, 2004). In addition, substance abusers with PDs, especially Antisocial Personality Disorder, are likely to be viewed and managed inconsistently by treatment professionals (Fishbein, 2004; MacKay, 1986). This is due, in part, to vast differences in training and varying treatment philosophies often seen in chemical dependency specialists. For example, the authors have observed countless counselors who insist that chemical abuse *causes* what "appears to be" antisocial personality disorder. If the chemical abuse is successfully treated, their reasoning goes, the antisocial behavior will disappear. Likewise, prominent sociological and criminological theories attempting to explain criminal behavior assume that the fundamental *cause* of antisocial behavior rests in society, parenting, problematic life experiences, or economic conditions. This assertion has, no doubt, some validity; however, as stated earlier, such assumptions are of limited value within the day-to-day operation of criminal justice treatment.

The essential problem with these views is that none of them encapsulates the totality of the problem. In fact, the focus on society, early life issues, or economic conditions as the underlying cause of criminal behavior has sometimes proven to undermine genuine treatment. The reason for this is that each of these explanatory ideas makes something *outside* the individual in question as the cause of his or her criminal behavior. Some argue that the focus on society simply gives substance-abusing offenders an excuse. In his now-classic book, *Inside the Criminal Mind*, Stanton Samenow (1984; pp. 5-6) wrote: "We ask 'why' to make sense out of a vicious, illegal, unprovoked act..." He continues, "...our current thinking about the cause of crime is dead wrong..." and adds, "We must understand how criminals think and realize that they have a fundamentally different view of the world ... criminals cause crime—not bad neighborhoods, inadequate parents, television, schools, drugs, or unemployment. Crime resides within the minds of human beings and is not caused by social conditions."

Samenow's assertion should be seen as a somewhat extreme viewpoint in and of itself. It was made in an era when the dominant causal theories of criminal behavior pointed to society as the culprit in an attempt to put the focus on the criminal rather than society. It was put forth prior to increasingly sophisticated genetic research and also without an understanding of how crime might be *escalated* by drug use or escalated by debilitating social conditions. Fishbein (2004) wrote, "As a phenomenon to be studied, 'antisocial behavior' is a complex concept ... [and] a longstanding or recurrent pattern of antisocial behavior is likely due to the cumulative, developmental influence of interacting biological and environmental factors" (pp. 5-6).

Personality Disorders are considered by many professionals to be the most researched of all psychological and psychiatric diagnoses (Gunderson, 1983; Hilsenroth, Hibbard, Nash, & Handler, 1993; Widiger, Frances, Spitzer, & Williams, 1988) and Antisocial Personality Disorder (ASPD) in particular has been the focus of an amazingly vast amount of research (Fishbein, 2004). In view of the substantial body of literature on PDs, it is surprising that many who treat substance abusers with coexisting PDs attempt to treat the substance abuse as a separate problem in the belief that substance abuse causes antisocial behavior or that the antisocial behavior will cease when substance abuse ceases. In addition, it is also remarkable that inappropriate counseling and treatment methods continue to be applied to antisocial abusers in the belief or hope that antisocial abusers will respond favorably to traditional mental health, educational, and other counseling interventions. Many counselors still persist in using client-centered counseling approaches, believing that helping the offenders "understand their feelings" will somehow reduce offending. With a few notable exceptions (discussed in detail later), it is well documented and accepted that almost all therapeutic interventions with antisocial substance abusers fail to reduce their substance abuse or antisocial behavior, *and some approaches actually increase offending* (Fishbein, 2004). However, during the past decade, focused treatment interventions have been devised, tested, and researched—this indicates that some substance abusers with Antisocial Personality Disorder (ASPD) can be successfully treated thereby leading to significant declines in both substance abuse and antisocial behavior. In particular, cognitive-behavioral and behavioristic-oriented approaches have been effective with ASPD abusers because they attempt to treat the core issues of ASPD rather than only treat its associated symptoms (e.g. substance use and abuse). Thus, effective interventions for the ASPD client must take into account the unique personality characteristics and defense mechanisms displayed by these clients while also motivating and facilitating clients to change. Understanding the dynamics and thought processes of ASPD clients is an essential component for successful treatment of the symptoms of ASPD. This text serves as an introduction to the history and development of treatments for ASPD and provides current insights and developments in effectively treating ASPD.

Background & History
of Antisocial Personality Disorder

Many professionals tend to view ASPD as synonymous with criminal behavior and "criminal personality." Although the large majority of criminals are diagnosable with ASPD, not all are. Likewise, some individuals with diagnosable ASPD are not criminals but they do share certain traits and behavioral patterns with other ASPDs. In addition, most substance abusers and about half of all alcoholics who enter treatment are also diagnosable as having ASPD or one of its associated personality disorders. Programs, however, are hesitant to label their clients with the diagnosis. (This is due, in part, to the long-standing tradition of third party payers denying claims with ASPD as the primary diagnosis.) Thus, there is a great overlap between substance abuse, alcoholism, and ASPD that has long been recognized and studied. An understanding of the modern ASPD diagnosis begins with a discussion of the terms *psychopath* and *sociopath*, which have been utilized by many to describe the criminal personality.

Genesis Of The Terms Psychopath & Sociopath

In the 18th and 19th centuries, early clinicians like Pinel and Rush speculated that criminal conduct, immoral behavior, drug use, and alcoholism were forms of mental illness. In 1835, the term *"moral insanity"* was first used by psychiatrist J. C. Prichard to describe "perverted or depraved" behavior stemming from a mental derangement without apparent intellectual problems. In the late 1800s the term *"psychopath"* was applied to such persons because it was believed that a hereditary influence caused the disorder (Davidson, 1956). In the 20th century, the term *"sociopath"* was increasingly used (Overholser & Owens, 1961) because of two factors. The first factor was that the sociopath aimed his or her behavior against society's laws and mores. Secondly, it was believed that social conditions played a large part in the development of sociopathic behavior (Bootzin & Acocella, 1984). Partridge (1930) introduced the term *sociopath.*

When psychological diagnosis was revised in 1952 by the American Psychiatric Association, ASPD was placed under sociopathic personality disturbances in support of the recognition of the role of society in its development. The sociopathic personality in the diagnostic revision of 1952 had a number of related subgroups including alcoholism, drug addiction, and other dyssocial and antisocial reactions.

Despite the lack of understanding and controversy surrounding its causes, sociopathic disorder was absorbed into psychopathology as a "character" or "personality" disorder. At the same time, there was agreement that alcoholism, drug addiction, and sociopathic behavior were related disorders. Later, the Personality Disorders and substance abuse disorders were completely separated, although it was recognized that many of those with PDs had substance abuse problems and many substance abusers had PDs. Unfortunately, the separation of Personality Disorders from substance abuse disorders has led some to conclude that the two problems are truly separate and distinct. Character and personality disorders are not typically considered to be a "disease," illness, or psychosis. They are inappropriate, dysfunctional behavioral patterns and personality styles. Perhaps the most accurate way to describe PDs is that they are *disorders*. In 1957 the *American Psychiatric Association's Psychiatric Glossary* defined the psychopath as:

> "a person whose behavior is predominantly amoral or antisocial and characterized by impulsive, irresponsible actions satisfying only immediate and narcissistic interests without concern for obvious and implicit social consequences, accompanied by minimal outward evidence of anxiety or guilt."

Therefore, the habitual criminal was considered a type of sociopath just like many alcoholics and drug addicts since their antisocial behavior affected many others. This categorization has always been found to have limited usefulness. As a result, efforts to better diagnose sociopaths continued. At the same time, an effort to separate alcoholism and substance dependence from personality and character disorders occurred.

The first *Diagnostic and Statistical Manual (DSM)* of the American Psychiatric Association in 1960 began to divide sociopaths into two categories and placed substance abuse diagnoses into a major diagnostic group termed "Axis I." The *DSM-III* later divided antisocials into two categories: 1) those who have had an enduring pattern of antisocial behavior from childhood or adolescence, and 2) those who appear to have begun antisocial behavior in adulthood (after age 18) (Bootzin & Acocella, 1984).

"We must understand how criminals think and realize that they have a fundamentally different view of the world ... criminals cause crime ... Crime resides within the minds of human beings and is not caused by social conditions." Stanton Samenow (1984)

Understanding Psychiatric Diagnosis—
The 5 Axes

The modern *DSM-IV-TR*, the *Diagnostic and Statistical Manual of Mental Disorders—IV (Text Revision)* of the American Psychiatric Association (5th Edition - 2000, Revised), divides disorders into 5 Axes. The Axes are intended to allow practitioners a way to organize and diagnose mental disorders and specify one's functioning level in a practical and useful schemata. It is necessary to mention that while the Axes may prove helpful to treatment professionals, allow those performing diagnosis to be exceedingly specific, and promote specific coding numbers for third-party payers, the methodology can be nearly incomprehensible for those outside the fields of psychology and psychiatry. A brief explanation of the Axes follows:

Axis I is reserved for all psychiatric diagnoses with the exceptions of personality disorders and mental retardation. Common examples in Axis I would be schizophrenia, depression, bipolar disorder (or using old terminology, manic-depressive), alcoholism, and anxiety disorders. Note that substance use and abuse disorders are Axis I, with the exception of drug overdose diagnoses, which are Axis III. (Drug overdose is a medical condition.)

Axis II is utilized for diagnosing developmental disorders starting in infancy or childhood. These include mental retardation and the personality disorders. Axis II diagnoses (except mental retardation) are typically not *fully* made when an individual is also diagnosed with an Axis I disorder. For example, if an individual is diagnosed with major depression (an Axis I diagnosis), it is possible that antisocial behavior could be a result of the depression. The thinking is that a true evaluation of the individual's personality and behavior cannot be made until the individual is no longer suffering from depression. In this case, the diagnosis of a personality disorder is "deferred," meaning that if the antisocial behavior persists after the depression lifts, then the personality disorder diagnosis can be fully made. Thus, many treatment programs treat alcoholism and substance abuse disorders under the assumption that antisocial personality will disappear when the substance use is treated. In reality, such programs release their clients immediately after substance abuse treatment meaning that the "deferred" Axis II diagnosis is never revisited. On the other hand, the criminal justice system encounters offenders who were previouslyand frequently treated for substance abuse. Yet the diagnosis of ASPD is often again "deferred" because Axis I disorders (alcoholism and/or substance abuse) take priority. In essence, this cycle leads many to the conclusion that many offenders are "substance abusers"—not ASPD afflicted individuals.

Axis III is reserved for most general medical conditions, especially those that might exacerbate a psychological problem. For example, diabetes or Alzheimer's disease can cause physiological symptoms leading to unusual and abnormal behavior; thus, knowledge of the active medical conditions is crucial to having a full understanding of the behavior associated with a mental condition. Drug overdose episodes and withdrawal are included in Axis III as medical conditions.

Axis IV is reserved for psychosocial and environmental problems. Poverty, homelessness, job skills, education, and dysfunctional families are examples. The inclusion of Axis IV allows for more detailed treatment plans.

Axis V is a Global Assessment of Functioning Scale, which is used to rate the individual's ability to cope with "normal" life. The scale goes to 100; for example, a low score of 10 indicates danger to self and/or others while a high score of 100 indicates superior functioning in a wide range of activities.

Psychopaths & Extremes of ASPD

Today, the term *psychopath* is used predominantly from a psychodynamic viewpoint but is utilized by a growing segment of criminal justice specialists. Persons labeled psychopathic are typically considered "mean, criminal, manipulative, or sometimes entrepreneurial" — a practice that has lead to some misunderstanding and treatment ineffectiveness (Reid, 1985). The current use of the term *psychopath* is addressed in a later section; however, it is increasingly being more widely employed in criminal justice settings. The easiest way to understand the application of the term *psychopath* is to see it as existing on a graduated scale like a thermometer. Most people understand the word "hot" when it comes to temperature but there are varying degrees of hot. Most people agree that a temperature of 100 degrees is "hot" but they would also agree that the temperature on the surface of the sun is hot. They would also agree that there is a vast difference between the two. Consistent antisocial behavior can be labeled as antisocial personality, but as with the understanding of the term "hot," there are different degrees of psychopathy. That is, there are different degrees of psychopathy ranging from a low-grade psychopath (such as a petty thief) to an extreme psychopath (a serial killer).

Myers' introductory text, *Psychology* (1992), cites extreme ASPDs or psychopaths (e.g., Charles Manson) as clever con artists or serial killers. Many other criminals (who are also clearly antisocial) do not fit this extreme. The term *sociopath* is still used by some sociologists and criminologists. In common or popular usage, both terms (*psychopath* and *sociopath*) are often thought to be the most severe forms of criminal personalities. It is a common practice to view sociopaths and psychopaths as existing on a continuum from mild, to moderate, to extreme and to term their disorder ASPD. In other words, the three terminologies (*antisocial personality*, *sociopath*, and *psychopath*) are sometimes used interchangeably but practitioners often have slightly different definitions for each. In addition, scales that attempt to create a categorical score on psychopathy, sociopathy, or antisocial personality exist. Many of these have been most useful for research but their actual predictive ability is questionable.

That ASPDs create huge problems for society is unquestionable. The costs to society in crime, effects on victims, incarceration and apprehension, health costs of victims, families, and the perpetrator, substance abuser, and alcoholic is staggering. *The Comprehensive Textbook of Psychiatry* (Freedman, Kaplan, & Sadock, 1976) states that sociopaths comprise a small but quite costly segment of society because their behavior requires disproportionate attention. "From costly efforts to control and manage their childhood problems to criminal justice costs and added costs to society in taking care of their victims and their deserted families, society pays a disproportionate share" because of ASPDs (p. 1287).

Quick Facts—

• Personality Disorders are considered by many professionals to be the most researched of all psychological and psychiatric diagnoses.

• Having offenders "understand their feelings" will not reduce antisocial behavior.

• Most substance abusers and half of all alcoholics entering treatment have ASPD or a related personality disorder.

• Many people view ASPD and criminal personality as the same thing.

• The terms psychopath, sociopath, and Antisocial Personality Disorder overlap in meaning and can be considered to be synonomous.

Chapter 6

Characteristics of Antisocial Personality Disorder: Psychopathy vs. ASPD

Descriptions of Antisocial Personality Disorder have been amazingly consistent over time and have attempted to give an understanding of the core of the disorder. The textbook *Psychopathology* (Page, 1971) described ASPD as a diagnosis "... loosely applied to a heterogeneous group of individuals whose life style is marked by the immediate gratification of impulses and egocentric desires without regard or concern for the feelings and welfare of others" (p. 317). Page divided the pathological **behavior** of antisocials into three areas: "... sociopaths may engage in unethical, immoral, or criminal behavior" (p. 317). One important issue that should be noted in the three behavioral areas Page listed is that not all Antisocials are criminals. The term "functional sociopath" is sometimes anecdotally applied to people who manage to stay within the bounds of the law while taking advantage of others in the performance of certain occupations. This might seem almost illogical but the following example illustrates how it occurs. Some automobile sales people, especially used car dealers, can say virtually anything about a specific car in order to get the buyer to the final steps of a

---

Sociopaths may engage in unethical, immoral, or criminal behavior, but not all who are diagnosed with ASPD are criminals.

---

purchase. The final step, of course, is the signing of a document that absolves the salesperson's pitch by specifically stating that nothing verbal counts after the document is signed. Note however, that the example does not apply to everyone in such an occupation. There are other occupations that conduct business in similar ways—ways that allow almost anything stated verbally, but in the final analysis, only what is on paper actually counts.

Page (1971) summarizes those with ASPD as a diverse group: "They have no sense of loyalty or responsibility... Other people are regarded as dupes or suckers, to be used and exploited. Successful [ASPDs] may be quite charming, persuasive, and socially adroit. When caught in some misdeed, they may skillfully extricate themselves by lying, blaming others (including the victim), begging forgiveness, and making a show of remorse. The true sociopath, however, does not experience genuine anxiety, guilt, or remorse for the anguish and suffering he causes others. Punishment has no deterrent effect. All that is learned from past experience is to be more circumspect next time" (p. 317). Page also cites impulsiveness, low frustration tolerance, lack of empathy, thrill seeking, and egocentricity as typical common characteristics of ASPD.

Noyes' Modern Clinical Psychiatry (Kolb, 1968) cites the ASPDs' often irritable, arrogant, and unyielding attitudes and behavior going on to say that they are rarely genuinely remorseful. "Frequently they show a rebellious attitude toward authority and society. ... They are cynical, devoid of a sense of honor or of shame, and are lacking in sympathy, affection, gratitude, or other social and esthetic sentiments. ... Many take pleasure in their struggle with the law and feel pride in their accomplishments. ... Punishments are considered as expressions of injustice and have no deterrent effect" (p. 505). Kolb's text addition-

---

The true sociopath does not experience genuine anxiety, guilt, or remorse and punishment has no deterrent effect. Antisocials care about satisfying their immediate needs.

ally states that the ASPD will *conveniently* forget events ("profess amnesia"), and often display extreme emotional outbursts to gain sympathy and impress observers (p. 506).

Freedman, *et al.* (1975) stated that antisocials tend to care about satisfying only their immediate needs and that they are characterized by hedonism and narcissism. They are incapable of maintaining meaningful relationships. Antisocials do not experience deep emotions but have great ability to pick apart feelings. Antisocials understand shame and guilt but do not actually experience them. The disorder begins in childhood or adolescence and tends to affect many areas in their lives.

More modern textbooks amplify earlier statements regarding ASPD: "the person [with ASPD] is typically a male whose lack of conscience becomes plain before age 15, as he begins to lie, steal, fight, or display unrestrained sexual behavior. In adulthood, he may be unable to keep a job, be irresponsible as a spouse and parent, and be assaultive or otherwise criminal. When the antisocial personality combines a keen intelligence with amorality, the result may be a clever con artist...; antisocial personalities feel little and fear little." (David Myers' *Psychology,* 1992; p. 471). Gunderson (1995) related: "Persons with the disorder believe that others, like themselves, are governed by coercion or personal profit ... and believe that, to survive, they need to extort whatever they can. That mind-set is usually manifest in unlawful behaviors ... such acts are done for self-serving purposes, such as profit, without regard for the effects on others" (pp. 1144-5).

The *DSM-II* summarized ASPDs thusly: "They are incapable of significant loyalty to individuals, groups, or social values. They are grossly selfish, callous, irresponsible, impulsive, and unable to feel guilt or to learn from experience or punishment. Frustration tolerance is low. They tend to blame others or offer plausible rationalization for their behavior."

In her classic book, *Deviant Children Grown Up: A Sociological and Psychiatric Study of Sociopathic Personality* (1966), L. N. Robins outlined the most common childhood symptoms predictive of adult ASPD. Much of this classic research (listed below) has been employed in formulating the diagnostic criteria for the disorder and the descriptions are considered to remain accurate. The number following the symptom is the percent of ASPD diagnosed adults who had the symptom during their childhood:

Theft (83%)
Incorrigibility (80%)
Truancy (66%)
Running away from home (65%)
Negative peers as companions (56%)
Physically aggressive (45%)
Impulsive (38%)
Reckless behavior (35%)
Irresponsible behavior (35%)
Slovenly appearance (32%)
Bedwetting (32%)
Lack of guilt (32%)
Pathological lying (26%)
Sexual perversions (18%)

Robins' classic work went on to tabulate the most common symptoms of adult antisocials. The number following the symptom is the percent of those with ASPD who have a significant problem in the respective life area:

Alcohol/Drug abuse (90%)
Problems with work (85%)
Marital problems (81%)
Financially dependent (79%)
Arrests (75%)
School/educational problems (71%)
Impulsive behavior (67%)
Sexual behavior (64%)
Vagrancy (60%)
Belligerence (58%)

Social isolation (56%)
Lack of guilt (40%)
Somatic complaints (31%)
Use of aliases (29%)
Pathological lying (16%)
Suicide attempts (11%)

It should be noted that *the connection between substance abuse and alcoholism has long been apparent in ASPDs.* Robins' (1966) study found that about 90% of ASPDs displayed such difficulties. These findings have also been verified in more recent times and are discussed elsewhere.

Researchers have found that ASPDs tend to display consistent, enduring personality characteristics. By *enduring* it is implied that the characteristics begin early in life and extend into adulthood. While not all of those with the disorder display all of the common characteristics, there is a consistent core of traits usually found. It is wise to keep in mind that the traits of ASPD exist in degrees much like a thermometer. Treatment professionals often expect to see the extremes of ASPD traits in antisocial clients; however, in actuality each of the common traits can vary from mild to extreme. This can cause some confusion for some treatment providers, especially those who work almost exclusively in settings likely to house large numbers of ASPDs. For example, many counselors who work in prison settings often come to view the offenders with more mild ASPD characteristics as *not* having ASPD because other offenders with extreme ASPD characteristics are also frequently observed in their setting, providing such a stark contrast. These extreme examples make the more mild ASPD offenders seem more "normal." It is appropriate to view ASPD on a graduated scale

---

The connection between ASPD and substance abuse/alcoholism has long been noted.

---

like a thermometer ranging from mild ASPD to extreme ASPD. Bursten (1972) characterized the more common core personality traits of ASPDs as:

Manipulative
Selfish
Egocentric
Callous
Irresponsible
Impulsive
Lack of guilt
Lack of genuine remorse
Fail to learn from experience
Fail to learn from punishment
Have low frustration tolerance
Blame others or society for their problems
Make excuses
Have superficial relationships
Produce conflict with their behavior

Probably the most respected and seminal work in studying ASPDs is Hervey Cleckley's *The Mask of Sanity* (1964). Cleckley's description is perhaps the most cited classic work even today, and almost every research study on ASPD has verified his profile of the antisocial personality. In his book, Cleckley listed the basic clinical profile of ASPD:

Superficial charm and apparent "intelligence"
Not delusional or clinically irrational
Unreliable
Insincere and untruthful
Lack of shame
Lack of remorse

Antisocial behavior occurs without appropriate motivation
Poor judgment
Failure to profit from experience
Egocentric
Lack of ability to love
Restricted repertoire of feelings
Lack and loss of insight
Lack of appropriate interpersonal responses
Acts out under the influence
Capable of acting out while sober
May attempt suicide but rarely carries out
Impersonal sex life
Has no life plan

DSM-IV-TR Diagnostic Criteria for ASPD

The *DSM-IV-Text Revised* (2000) section on Personality Disorders codes all PDs in Axis II. The Axis II criteria for ASPD refers to "a pervasive pattern of disregard for, and violation of, the rights of others that begins in childhood or early adolescence and continues into adulthood." The *DSM-IV-TR* is careful to state that ASPD represents a pattern of behavior over time showing that the person disregards others' rights. In addition, the *DSM-IV-TR* also notes that ASPD is sometimes referred to as *psychopathy, sociopathy*, or *dyssocial* disorder. Deceit and manipulation are listed as core elements of the disorder. The text stresses "it is essential in making the diagnosis to collect material from sources other than the individual being diagnosed."

ASPD is an *Axis II, Cluster B disorder* associated with the other Cluster B disorders. These are Borderline Personality Disorder, Histrionic Personality Disorder, and Narcissistic Personality Disorder. The other Cluster B disorders are briefly discussed later.

The assessment of ASPD requires that three initial findings be made prior to the actual diagnosis. First, the individual must be at least 18 years of age. Second, there must be some evidence of antisocial behavior before the age of 15, ideally with an earlier diagnosis of Con-

---

1. The individual must be at least 18.
2. There must be evidence of antisocial behavior before age 15.
3. ASPD cannot be diagnosed during active mania or schizophrenia.

---

duct Disorder (discussed later). Third, the diagnosis cannot be made during active mania or during a schizophrenic episode. If these three criteria are met, *at least three of the following seven items* must be found.

1) Fails to conform to social norms with respect to lawful behavior as evidenced by repeatedly behaving in ways that are grounds for arrest.

2) Displays deceit by repeatedly lying, use of aliases, or conning others for personal gain or pleasure.

3) Shows a pattern of impulsive behavior and/or fails to plan.

4) Displays irritability and aggressiveness displayed by fights or assaults.

5) Displays reckless disregard for self or others.

6) Shows consistent irresponsibility displayed by inconsistent work behavior and/or not honoring financial obligations.

7) Shows lack of remorse displayed by being indifferent to or rationalizing about hurting, mistreating, or stealing from others.

Item Explanations

A. Client Age

Since ASPD is a chronic, ongoing pattern of antisocial behavior since adolescence, the diagnosis requires that the client be at least 18 years old. Prior to age 18, clients displaying antisocial behavior are typically diagnosed as having Conduct Disorder or one of its related diagnoses. The related diagnoses include Oppositional/Defiant Disorder or Attention Deficit-Hyperactivity. Note that unusually early chemical use, including smoking, is one of the diagnostic criteria for Conduct Disorder. Conduct Disorder is discussed in more detail in Chapter 9.

B. Evidence of Conduct Disorder Prior to Age 15

Many adult ASPDs have not been diagnosed as having Conduct Disorder in their childhoods, and the actual diagnosis is not necessary for the diagnosis of ASPD to be made. Evidence of *some* aspects of Conduct Disorder is necessary. Some clinicians believe that in certain cases the lack of apparent childhood problems in adult ASPD individuals may be because of various factors that allowed the individual to escape detection. Adolescents can also occasionally be raised in surroundings that approve of childhood antisocial behaviors. In general, clinicians ask adult clients a series of questions designed to uncover whether antisocial behaviors were present in their adolescence in order to gain access to their juvenile information. Conduct Disorder will be addressed again; however, evidence of Conduct Disorder can be found if some of the following behaviors were present before age 15: fights, incidences of bullying, using a weapon, cruelty to animals or people, forcing sexual activity, theft or stealing, arson, repetitive vandalism, shoplifting, frequent deceit and lying, and problems at school or violating reasonable parental rules. As a rule, the behaviors must have caused some sort of problems in school, work, or their social life.

C. ASPD Cannot be Diagnosed During a Schizophrenic Episode or Manic Episode

Untreated schizophrenia can produce a wide range of bizarre and often unlawful behavior. It is not appropriate to assess an individual for ASPD during an active schizophrenic episode. This does not mean that schizophrenics cannot also have ASPD. It simply means that the behaviors the individual performs when the symptoms of schizophrenia are under control (usually through psychotropic medications) should be the primary focus. In addition, individuals with variations of Bipolar Affective Disorder (once called Manic Depression) cannot be assessed for ASPD during active manic episodes. Mania produces a host of bizarre behavior, which sometimes crosses over into unlawful actions.

D. Pattern of Antisocial Behavior Since Age 15 (must have only three or more of the following seven items to qualify):

1. A repeating pattern of performance of unlawful behaviors for which the individual could be arrested. This item obviously applies to many offenders, especially those who are not first-time offenders. In reality, the vast majority of those incarcerated in prisons are not true first-time offenders, as the current criminal justice system places virtually all genuine first offenders on some form of probation. Also, implied in the concept of "first-time offender" is the idea that it is the first time the individual has been arrested—not the first time the individual performed the behavior in question.

2. A pattern of lying and deceit is present. Deceit includes the use of aliases (false names). Using lies and manipulation to achieve money, pleasure, or other advantages are also typical.

3. A pattern of impulsive actions, including quitting jobs suddenly, traveling with no itinerary, moving and having no current address, or rapidly ending and starting new relationships.

4. A pattern of physical aggressiveness including fighting and assaults. This aspect of ASPD is often found in violent offenders and can be completely absent in others.

5. Lack of concern for others' safety or welfare including any of the following: child neglect/ abuse, high-risk sexual behavior, thrill-seeking behaviors, frequent driving while intoxicated, reckless driving, putting others at risk, or similar risky behaviors.

6. A pattern of irresponsibility regarding work, paying bills, or following through with important responsibilities. Periods of unemployment, job abandonment, failure to pay family support, or defaulting on debts or obligations are examples. The important issues in this aspect of ASPD are if the individual has steadily worked when it was expected and needed, worked when work was available, and the conditions under which the individual in question quit or abandoned jobs.

7. Lack of remorse or indifference to those people whom the person hurt. Making excuses, blaming the victim, minimizing harm, and failure to make amends are all examples.

Psychopathy vs. ASPD & Recidivism Prediction

The utilization of tests and assessment instruments in criminal justice has become a popular topic of research, and tests are theoretically useful methods that can aid decision-making in offender populations. The goals are to devise a tool that can accurately determine who should be placed into treatment programs based on need, who will best respond to treatment, as well as predicting future recidivism and violence. The assignment of offenders to different types of probation, drug court programs, or institutional programs is, in part, done by combining background information with a variety of assessments. The issue is fraught with legal and ethical considerations. The reliability and validity of specific tests are both important components that must be present for a test to be found useful. A host of instruments have been devised and researched, but the construct of *psychopathy*—as opposed to ASPD—has become a major focal point for many. Psychologist Robert D. Hare (1996) is the leading proponent of using the term *psychopathy* with offender populations. Hare argues that there should be a distinction between ASPD and psychopathy because the diagnosis of ASPD relies on some clinical inference and judgment, while the issue of psychopathy supposedly focuses more on behavior. That is, Hare asserts that the diagnosis of ASPD results in a diagnosis with good reliability but "dubious validity." He argues that the diagnosis of ASPD leads to individuals with completely different personalities sharing the same diagnosis. Hare's goal has been to operationalize the term *psychopathy* by creating a structured tool to assess it in individuals and then give a numerical score that can be used for prediction of future violence, recidivism, and program placement.

In 1980 Hare devised his first checklist in an attempt to provide an "operational definition" for psychopathy in offenders. The checklist was subsequently revised and several versions exist today. *The Hare Psychopathy Checklist—revised* (PCL-R), has 20 items and another commonly-used version has 12 items. The diagnostic tool is utilized in a structured interview with each item rated from 0 to 2. Scores in the PCL-R range from 0 to 40. Hare places the general cutoff score indicating psychopathy when the total score reaches 30, and he has found that 15-20 percent of offenders reach that score. The items on the checklist include: superficiality and glibness, overly high self-appraisal, lack of remorse and empathy, deceit and manipulation, pathological lying, promiscuity, adult and adolescent behavior problems, impulsivity, and irresponsibility. The test is utilized by trained personnel and obviously relies on some clinical inference and judgment, just as the diagnosis of ASPD requires. However, the PCL-R results in a numerical score.

Hare's research has found that "most individuals with ASPD are not psychopaths" and believes that the diagnosis of ASPD has limited usefulness. On the other hand, it is argued that psychopathy scores can be used for predictive purposes and for treatment decisions. As related more fully in a later section, the newer concepts of "treatment responsivity," "criminal risk," and "criminogenic needs" that are now widely employed in criminal justice treatment have direct relevance to the possible utilization of the psychopathy scale and scores. In brief, if the test could validly and reliably predict who most needs treatment, who would respond and benefit most to treatment, and who would likely recidivate, it would be highly useful.

Research has supported some of Hare's hypotheses and evaluated a wide range of possible uses. While hundreds of research studies have been done on the construct of psychopathy, only a few will be cited. One study (Lynam, et al., 2005) found that psychopathy was a valid construct with male juveniles. Another (Birbaumer, et al., 2005) compared two groups. One group consisted of 10 male psychopaths identified by high scores on the PCL-R while the other was a matched group of 10 non-psychopath controls. Differences in brain function, measured by magnetic resonance imaging, was the focus. The results showed that the controls showed high activation in the limbic system during fear conditioning while the psychopathic group showed no such activation. (This will become more meaningful in a later chapter.) In a study of nearly 700 American jail inmates (Walsh, Swogger, & Kosson, 2004), PCL-R scores were found to be significantly predictive of violent behavior. In a meta-analysis of 21 studies containing nearly 9,000 offenders, substance abusers, and mental health clients (Skeem, et al., 2004) PCL-R scores for blacks and whites were compared. Results showed that the two racial groups did not differ in psychopathy. Another study (Douglas, et al., 2005) found that PCL-R scores were "meaningfully" related to aggression, substance abuse, and personality disorders.

The use of the PCL-R as a predictive or diagnostic tool is not without its detractors or studies that question its validity. Kroner, Mills, & Reddon (2005) conducted a study with 1,614 individuals. They employed four tests: the PCL-R, the Level of Service Inventory-Revised, Violence Risk Appraisal Guide, and the General Statistical Information on Recidivism measure to predict future recidivism. In addition, the researchers created four other instruments by randomly combining items from the tests. Results showed that "the original instruments did not improve prediction over randomly structured scales, nor did the restructuring of items improve risk assessment, suggesting substantial deficiencies in the conceptualization of risk assessment and instrumentation."

Freedman (2001) is a major critic of the PCL-R's use as a predictive and diagnostic tool. Freedman's historical review related that in 1983 the U.S. Supreme Court noted that clinical judgment of future dangerousness was "generally inaccurate" leading to the creation of a "new science" for predicting violence based on assessments that gave scores. He cites four studies that had to utilize different cutoff scores on the PCL-R, ranging from 19 to 30, to make statistically significant predictions. The major problem with the cutoff scores on the PCL-R, Freedman argues, is false positives. A false positive is when an individual is found to have a score indicating psychopathy but later does not recidivate or show violence. Nine studies are cited by Freedman with false positives found ranging from 50 to 75 percent. He argues, "Researchers, of course, see potential in the PCL-R in its ability to draw group distinctions—differentiating between psychopaths and non psychopaths." But he adds that Hare himself has cautioned that "A high PCL-R score is consistent with high risk, but a low score does not imply low risk." This implies that a high number of false negatives are also present. False negatives would be offenders who scored low on the PCL-R but later recidivated or were violent. A substantial number of studies have found that PCL-R scores do not correlate with violence or recidivism. In summarizing research on the actual predictive ability of the PCL-R on violence and recidivism, Freedman relates, "This means that the PCL-R is explaining 7% of the behaviors that it seeks to predict. The other 93% is unexplained or explained by something else entirely." In sum, he writes, "The PCL-R should not be used to predict future dangerousness in clinical or forensic settings at this time."

Attempts to predict future recidivism are important to criminal justice. Another commonly used assessment tool discussed later is the Level of Service Inventory—Revised (LSI-R), which attempts to measure a host of risk factors and needs. If a valid and reliable measure can be identified, appropriate levels of treatment could be applied, offenders could be assigned to the ideal level of supervision, and supervision efforts could be focused on those most likely to recidivate. In theory, this sounds great. However, as we discuss in a later chapter, given the actual level of recidivism in America's criminal justice system, it is far better to see every offender as a potential recidivist rather than being "low risk" for recidivism. This is because if the time frame for assessing future recidivism is long enough, meaning more than three years, the majority of offenders will recidivate.

If a valid and reliable measure can be identified, appropriate levels of treatment could be applied, offenders could be assigned to the ideal level of supervision, and supervision efforts could be focused on those most likely to recidivate.

Chapter 7

The Incidence of Antisocial Personality Disorder

Prior to extensive epidemiological research in the 1990s and 2000s that reliably determined the rate of various psychiatric diagnoses in the general population, estimates of the incidence of ASPD varied widely. Early research estimated the incidence of ASPD at between 1% to 15% of the population depending upon the region, locale, and demographics (see Freedman, *et al.*, 1976 for a review). Rosenthal (1970) reviewed research on the prevalence of ASPD and cited data estimating that between .05% to 15% of the population had the disorder. The sequence of *DSM*s has consistently placed the incidence of ASPD at around 3% of the adult population with men outnumbering women about eight to one. Robins and Regier's (1991) major study conducted in the early 1990s, showed that 2.6% of the noninstitutionalized population was diagnosable as having ASPD. Of the noninstitutionalized men, 4.5% were diagnosable as having ASPD while noninstitutionalized women showed a rate of 0.8%. Among racial groupings, Robins and Regier found 2.3% of blacks, 2.6% of whites, and 3.4% of Latinos were diagnosable as having ASPD.

It should be noted that all of the research conducted on the incidence of ASPD and other disorders has been conducted on noninstitutionalized populations. Thus, the actual incidence of ASPD in the entire population would be somewhat higher. For example, in 1990 1,118,000 offenders were incarcerated during the time of Robins and Regier's study. As will be discussed later, about 80% of those who are incarcerated have ASPD. Thus, in 1990 the actual incidence of ASPD in the entire adult population would have been closer to 3%, with the rate among men being substantially higher than among women.

Probably the most extensive demographic data ever collected on the incidence of ASPD was first published in January 1994 in the *Archives of General Psychiatry* (Kessler, McGonagle, Zhao, Nelson, Hughes, Eshleman, Whittchen, & Kendler, 1994). In this study, the first of its kind, the prevalence of all *DSM-III-R* diagnoses in the adult, noninstitutionalized population was collected by interviewers from all states from over 8,000 subjects. Conducted as the *National Comorbidity Survey,* the Kessler, *et al.* study is considered to be one of the most accurate of all such studies. This study showed that 5.8% of male adults had ASPD while 1.2% of females had ASPD. Overall, 3.5% of the population had ASPD.

A series of *National Comorbidity Survey* replications were conducted in the mid-2000s on differing samples. One of these (National Institutes of Health, 2005) examined 43,000 American adults and showed that 3.6 percent of noninstitutionalized adults were diagnosable with ASPD. Another study (Grant, *et al.*, 2004) revealed that 14.8 percent of adults had at least one personality disorder with 3.63 percent of adults diagnosable with ASPD. In summary, with institutionalized ASPDs added to the totals, it can reliably be estimated that 4.2% of the population has ASPD (males at 5.8%, females at 1.9%).

ASPD—by Sex, Race, Age, Education, Income, & Marital Status

Virtually all studies show that males with ASPD far outnumber females with the disorder. In a study of over 43,000 adults, Grant, *et al.* (2004) found that the ASPD rate in males is 5.5 percent compared to 1.9 percent in females. The results also showed the prevalence of ASPD in racial groups: whites: 3.6 percent; blacks: 3.7 percent; Native American: 9.7 percent; Asian: 1.8 percent; and Latinos: 3.3 percent. When the relationship of ASPD to age was analyzed, the results showed what has long been observed in offender populations. ASPD incidence declines with age. The ASPD rate among those age 18-29 was 6.2 percent; 30-44 was 4.2 percent; 45-64 was 2.8 percen; and 65+ was 0.6 percent. Factors not included in this analysis is the observation that many extreme ASPD offenders who were incarcerated at the time of the study were not included and the often cited anecdotal observation that younger ASPD individuals live risky lives that can lead to early

Incidence of ASPD in the U. S. Population

The National Comorbidity Survey (Kessler, *et al.*, 1994) and several replications (NIH, 2005; Grant, *et al.*, 2004) investigated the incidence of psychiatric disorders in the noninstitutionalized adult American population. Results showed:

5.8 % of Adult Males Have ASPD
1.9 % of Adult Females Have ASPD

3.5 % of all American Adults Have ASPD
(Noninstitutionalized only)

Including Institutionalized Adults, the Total Incidence of ASPD in America's Adult Population is:
4.2 %

Replications of the National Comorbidity Survey (Grant, *et al.*, 2004) have indicated that 14.8 % of America's adults have at least one Personality Disorder.

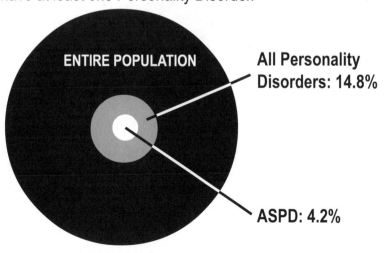

ENTIRE POPULATION

All Personality
Disorders: 14.8%

ASPD: 4.2%

death. This observation may be more related to the abuse of drugs by ASPDs than the ASPD itself. For example, Fridell & Hesse (2006) found that 15 years after drug detoxification and treatment, 24 percent of those treated were dead. The highest rates of ASPD are also found in those earning less than $35,000 per year and in those with less than a high school diploma. Additionally, the highest rates of ASPD are found in those who have been "never married."

ASPD & Offenders

In the initial chapter it was revealed that 3.2 percent of the adult population was under some sort of criminal justice supervision at any given time and that males comprise the large bulk of offenders. It is not a coincidence that somewhere between 3.7 to 4 percent of the adult

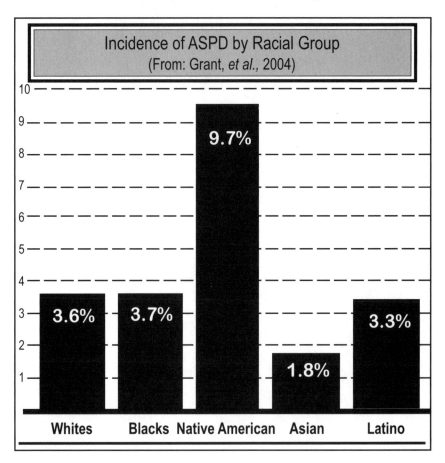

Incidence of ASPD by Racial Group
(From: Grant, et al., 2004)

population has ASPD. The fact that African Americans show an ASPD rate virtually identical to whites has been replicated in many other studies. And as mentioned in the prior chapter, tests of psychopathy show that blacks and whites show similar results. However, the earlier-cited statistics indicating that one of every 15 black males is incarcerated— as compared to only one of every 106 white males—gives one pause. While there obviously are several reasons for the discrepancy, it is apparent that the disproportionate incarceration of blacks is not due to a higher rate of ASPD or higher levels of psychopathy.

In *The Chemically Dependent Criminal Offender* (1993), relapse prevention specialist Terrence Gorski cited reliable figures indicating that 100% of the incarcerated prisoner population are drug and/ or alcohol users and 70% have serious (dependency) problems with drugs and alcohol. Gorski also cites figures stating that *nearly 100% of incarcerated offenders have ASPD or another related Personality Disorder.* Gorski and others view ASPD as a "criminal personality" that overlaps with chemical abuse. Substantial research has been conducted on the *DSM* criteria applied to offender populations. Virtually all research tends to yield figures showing that between 76% (Hare, 1980)

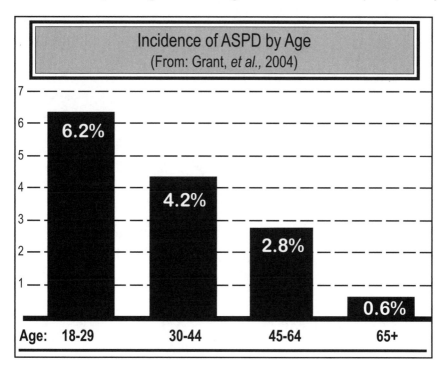

Incidence of ASPD by Age
(From: Grant, *et al.*, 2004)

to 80% (Guze, Goodwin, & Crane, 1969) of all offenders have ASPD. Hare, *et al.* (1991) cites research indicating that in 1990, the Correctional Service of Canada found that 75% of all male adults incarcerated in Canada had ASPD. It may be wise to state that the other 20% or so of offenders that are *not* ASPD diagnosable, often have another diagnosis. Depression, retardation, other PDs, and various psychoses comprise the diagnoses in the bulk of the remaining offenders.

One problem in diagnosing offenders for ASPD is the "deferred diagnosis" mentioned previously. A large majority of offenders have diagnosable substance or alcohol abuse problems (Axis I), which means that the diagnosis of ASPD (Axis II) would be "deferred" and ideally "revisited" after successful treatment. In reality, a diagnosis is seldom revisited or redone after treatment nor is it done prior to an offender leaving criminal justice supervision. In summary, criminal justice treatment professionals generally agree that the large bulk of incarcerated offenders, as well as a substantial proportion of those in other levels of criminal justice supervision, have diagnosable ASPD.

Quick Facts—

• ASPD is found in about 4.2 percent of the total adult population.

• The ASPD rate in men is 5.8 percent compared to 1.9 percent in women.

• The ASPD rate in blacks and whites is virtually identical, 3.7 percent and 3.6 percent, respectively.

• ASPD is related to age with the odds of ASPD decreasing as one ages beyond 29 and 44 years.

• ASPD is found in large numbers (76-80 percent) of offenders.

Chapter 8

Related Personality Disorders: In Brief

There are numerous personality disorders listed in the various versions of the *DSM*. However, those most relevant in criminal justice and substance abuse treatment are found in Cluster B, the category in which ASPD is found. Several other Cluster B Personality Disorders are frequently seen in substance abuse treatment and also in criminal justice clients. These would be most relevant in institutional and outpatient mental health programs and substance abuse treatment. Borderline PD, Histrionic PD, and Narcissistic PD are often encountered, with Borderline the most often seen of these in criminal justice populations. While each is diagnostically viewed as a separate, distinct category, it is also clear that they are a related cluster. In a paper reviewing research on *DSM-III-R* Personality Disorders (Jovanovic, Svrakic, & Tosevski, 1993), the relationship was made clear: *"...many PDs, classified as separate nosologic units, reflect different behavioral expression of the same personality deviation or co-occurring endpoints of the same pathogenesis"* (p. 559; emphasis added).

Borderline PD (BPD)

BPD is characterized by unstable and rapidly changing patterns of mood, relationships, self-image, and identity. It typically begins by early adulthood. Fear of abandonment, rejection, or loss of structure (real or perceived) in life are all possible components of the disorder. Self-image is unstable and dramatic shifts in goals, values, career, or sexual behavior/orientation may occur. Gambling, reckless spending, binge eating, substance abuse, and reckless behavior are typically seen.

BPD clients can make frequent suicide gestures, and self-mutilation are often observed. The diagnosis of BPD requires that at least five of the following nine behaviors be present:

1. Frantic efforts to avoid abandonment by others (real or imagined)

2. Unstable and intense personal relationships varying from idealization and devaluation.

3. Unstable self-image.

4. Impulsivity in at least two areas such as spending, sex behavior, reckless driving, or binge eating.

5. Recurring suicidal behavior or gestures.

6. Instability of mood, shifting rapidly over days including euphoria, irritability, and anxiety.

7. Feelings of emptiness.

8. Inappropriate anger, temper, or fights.

9. Quickly occurring or quickly dissipating paranoid thoughts.

Incidence of BPD. According to the *DSM-IV-TR* about 75 percent of those with BPD are female. It is estimated that about 2% of the adult population has the disorder. BPD is frequently encountered in female offender populations and is often an issue in domestic violence treatment. BPD may be found in rates from 10 to 20 percent in mental health treatment programs.

Histrionic PD (HPD)

Histrionic Personality Disorder (HPD) also typically begins by early adulthood. The disorder is characterized by extremes of emotion and attention-seeking behavior. The person afflicted with HPD is anxious, angry, or uncomfortable unless he or she is the center of attention.

Borderline Personality Disorder is seen in higher numbers in female offenders and in mental health treatment programs. Females comprise 75 percent of those with BPD.

They can be dramatic and flirtatious. Often they are seductive and provocative but are influenced by authority figures and fads. The diagnosis of HPD requires that five or more of the following eight characteristics be present:

1. Is uncomfortable when not the center of attention.

2. Is inappropriately sexually seductive or displays provocative behavior.

3. Emotions shift rapidly and are shallowly expressed.

4. Frequently uses physical appearance as attention-seeking behavior.

5. Speech that provides little detail but is strongly worded.

6. Emotion is expressed dramatically or in an exaggerated style.

7. Easily influenced by circumstances or by other people.

8. Sees relationships as more intimate or closer than they actually are.

Incidence of HPD. It is estimated that about 2.5% of the adult population has diagnosable HPD. The *DSM-IV-TR* relates that females may have a slightly higher incidence of HPD than males and that the rate of HPD in mental health settings is as high as 10-15 percent.

Narcissistic PD (NPD)

Narcissistic Personality Disorder (NPD), as do the other Cluster B disorders, begins by early adulthood. It is characterized by grandiosity, hypersensitivity, egocentricity, and lack of empathy. Those with NPD feel superior to others and have an inflated sense of self-importance while devaluing the importance of others.

The diagnosis of NPD is made when five or more of the following nine characteristics are present:

1. Grandiose sense of self-importance.

2. Preoccupied with fantasies of success, power, brilliance, beauty, or ideal love.

3. Believes he or she is special or unique and can only be understood by high-status people.

4. Needs to have excessive admiration.

5. Has a sense of entitlement.

6. Takes advantage of and exploits others.
7. Lacks empathy.
8. Is either envious of others or believes that others are envious.
9. Is arrogant or haughty.

Incidence of NPD. It is estimated that about 1% of the adult population has diagnosable NPD with more than half of these being males.

Chapter 9

Juveniles & Conduct Disorder

Adult ASPD is usually preceded by a distinct set and pattern of anti-social behaviors during late childhood and adolescence. A key word here is *pattern*. Research has shown that most males (90% to 94%) and most females (65% to 90%) have committed at least *one* delinquent act prior to age 18 (Snyder & Sickmund, 1995; p. 49 for a review). One delinquent act does not necessarily imply a pattern of behavior. However, the same research has shown that about 30% of males and less than 10% of females had performed *three* delinquent acts by their 18th year of age. Thus, it is true that most adolescents normally engage in some delinquent behavior; however, far fewer engage in a *pattern* of delinquent behavior.

The *DSM-IV* stated that the range of incidence of conduct disorder in males is 6% to 16% with urban areas showing a higher level. The range for females is 2% to 9%. The *DSM-IV-TR* relates that research results on Conduct Disorder vary widely from just one percent to well over 10 percent. Symptoms of conduct disorder are often seen in children as young as 6 years old; however, by age 16, those who have conduct disorder will have displayed its characteristic pattern of unconcern for others' rights and property and deceit/manipulation.

The rate of Conduct Disorder in males is 6 to 16 percent; the rate for females is 2 to 9 percent. The symptoms of Conduct Disorder can be seen by age 6, but by age 16 those with the disorder will display its characteristics.

Diagnostic Criteria of Conduct Disorder

Conduct Disorder can be of several types including Childhood-Onset (before age 10) or Adolescent-Onset (after age 10). The diagnosis is typically made as being Mild, Moderate, or Severe. The major descriptive features include behaviors and attitudes typical of ASPD such as little empathy and lack of concern for others. Aggression, lack of guilt and remorse, and blaming others for misdeeds are common. When tests of self-esteem are employed on children, those with Conduct Disorder may actually score high, which is interpreted as overly inflated. However, it is often paradoxically theorized that their "actual" self-esteem is low. This observational finding is both complex and controversial and may better be understood as flaws in self-esteem tests commonly utilized, or as a fundamental flaw in our construct of precisely what "self-esteem" means.

The initial observation of behaviors deemed as central to Conduct Disorder typically appear before age 16. It is important to note that the majority of those displaying the symptoms usually change by adulthood. However, nearly all adults with ASPD will have displayed the symptoms of Conduct Disorder.

Conduct Disorder is diagnosed when a pattern of behavior wherein the basic rights of others are violated and/or when age-appropriate norms and rules are violated. There are four categories of such behavior, and the diagnosis requires that at least three criteria within these be met within the past year and at least one must have occurred in the past 6 months. The four categories follow below with the specific behaviors listed in each.

1. Aggression—bullies, threatens, or intimidates; initiates fights; has used a weapon, cruelty to people, cruelty to animals; stolen through force; has forced sexual activity.

2. Property Destruction—deliberately set fires to cause serious damage; deliberately destroyed property in other ways.

3. Deceit or Theft—has broken into a car, building, or house; lies to obtain favors or goods; has shoplifted, committed forgery, stolen items.

4. Rules Violations—often stays out at night against parental prohibition; runs away from home overnight at least twice or once for an extended time; frequent truancy.

Conduct Disorder & Substance Abuse

One observation consistently made about children and adolescents that display conduct disorder symptoms is that they also tend to abuse drugs/ alcohol. In recent years a substantial amount of research has been conducted on this observation. Van Kamen & Loeber (1994), for example, evaluated the relationship between drug use and crime in 506 urban males. Their results showed that property crime patterns preceded drug usage. As the youth then began using drugs, their pattern and severity of crime tended to escalate. Research sponsored by the National Institute of Drug Abuse (Swan, 1993) has shown the same. NIDA research has indicated that "conduct disorder is in large part the common forerunner of both drug abuse and criminality, challenging the assumption that drug use causes crime" (p. 6). In a study (Freucht, Stephens, & Walker, 1994) discussed earlier, only 7.4% of all juvenile arrestees admitted to ever using cocaine. Urinalysis testing indicated that 8% had cocaine metabolites in their bodies at the time of their arrest. However, the Cleveland study also performed hair analysis showing that *60% of the arrestees had used cocaine within the last 30 days.* Substance abuse is one of the most frequently observed dual diagnoses found in Conduct Disorder.

Conduct Disorder is a persistent pattern of behavior characterized by at least three of four types of behavior: aggression, property destruction, deceit or theft, or rules violations.

Chapter 10

Substance Abuse, Offenders, and ASPD: Does Drug Abuse Cause Crime?

Does drug use cause crime? The answer to this question is at the same time complex and simple. The answer is both yes and no, but obviously more explanation is needed. Drug abuse is usually—but not always—a crime in itself. Drinking to excess can become a crime under many circumstances, but in and of itself, it's not a crime. The use of illegal drugs or misuse of prescription drugs is illegal, and some individuals, albeit a relatively small percentage of all offenders, enter the system solely because of such use. For example, the 2005 Bureau of Justice Statistics report on Probation and Parole (Glaze & Palla, 2005) found that 26 percent of all probationers were charged with drug law violations. But of the more than 14 million arrests each year, just 13 percent are drug law violations. It can be said that drug use *is* often a crime, but that doesn't mean it *causes* crime.

To answer the main question, a series of counter questions could be asked: If drugs and alcohol did not exist, would any crime take place? Would there still be people who meet the criteria of ASPD and would these people engage in activity that is criminal? Would some people still be violent, would burglary and theft occur, would forgery occur, would car theft occur? Jumping ahead of the explanation, the answers to all of these is *yes*, but without the presence of drugs or alcohol, crime would occur to a somewhat lesser extent. Only the extent of the decrease is debatable.

Understanding the relationship between drugs and crime has to be placed into the context of the pervasiveness of drug use in American society. The 1994 *National Comorbidity Survey* (which was described in a prior chapter) addressed rates of alcoholism and substance dependence in America. That survey showed that in the last 12 months, 2.8% of the population was dependent on drugs while 7.2% was dependent on alcohol. A 2004 replication of the study (Kessler, *et al.*, 2004) showed that 9.4% of the general population had a substance abuse disorder with another 8.5% showing an alcohol-related disorder. In general, about 15% of the entire adult population has a diagnosable substance abuse disorder. (Keep in mind that there are some people in these statistics who have both a drug and alcohol disorder.) However, it is also known that by the time students are seniors in high school, 66% will have used alcohol and 45% will have used an illegal drug (University of Michigan, 2008). Thus, the majority of adults will have used alcohol and a

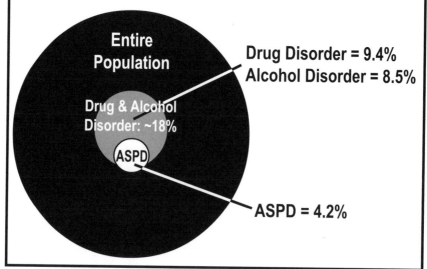

ASPD and Substance Abuse Disorders Overlap
(From: Kessler, *et al.*,1994; 2004)

The large majority of those diagnosable with ASPD—as well as offender populations—have a co-occurring substance abuse disorder. About half of all alcoholics who enter a treatment program have ASPD, but *less than half of all alcoholics have ASPD*. Alcoholics with ASPD are more likely to enter formal treatment programs, often because of coerced treatment due to an offense. Nearly all ASPDs who enter institutions or programs also have a chemical abuse disorder.

Entire
Population

Drug Disorder = 9.4%
Alcohol Disorder = 8.5%

Drug & Alcohol
Disorder: ~18%

ASPD

ASPD = 4.2%

substantial proportion—around half of the population—will have used some illegal drugs. In essence, most adults in America have used drugs or alcohol, often illegally or to excess, at least once. And most adults consume alcohol in widely varying amounts. The majority of the population uses drugs or alcohol, but the vast majority do not find their way into the criminal justice system.

By way of contrast, recall that a relatively small group, 3.2 percent of the adult population, is under some form of criminal justice supervision. Also recall that the vast majority of these individuals are diagnosable with ASPD. The 2004 ADAM study related that about 74% of arrestees had drugs and/or alcohol in their system at the time of arrest. Chapter 4 in this book related that between 70 to 100 percent of offenders had admitted drug problems. In essence, drug use and abuse, as well as alcohol use and abuse, are behaviors that ASPD-afflicted individuals gravitate toward, are attracted to, and engage in frequently. Remember that the very criteria employed in diagnosing both Conduct Disorder and ASPD involve risky behaviors including substance use. What this implies is that substance abuse and criminal activity—as well as the propensity to engage in criminal behavior—overlap each other. However, since the vast majority of people who have used and abuse drugs do not engage in crime beyond the actual use of the substances, something other than a causal relationship is present. Drug use—in and of itself—does not cause crime—but it is related to it. In brief, criminals are attracted to drug use. It's an activity they frequently engage in and often to excess. Obviously, many noncriminal people are also attracted to alcohol and, to a lesser extent, drugs. The difference in the two groups of substance users isn't really the amount consumed; it is the presence or absence of Antisocial Personality Disorder. In some

---

Only 3.2 percent of the adult population is under criminal justice supervision. We also know that the vast majority of these people abuse drugs and alcohol. Substance abuse, ASPD, and Conduct Disorder overlap.

ways this should now be obvious, but this has been confirmed by research investigating a key issue: Which comes first, the performance of deviant criminal behaviors or the use of drugs?

The abuse of drugs and alcohol is intimately connected to antisocial behavior and ASPD. The connection is not as direct as it may seem, however, and until recently it was unclear why some drug users and alcoholics performed crime and others didn't. Psychopharmacologist Oakley Ray's (Ray & Ksir, 1990) text, *Drugs, Society, & Human Behavior* stated that research had begun clarifying the relationship between deviance and drug use. Specifically they state that research indicates that ***deviance occurs first*** and ***drug use follows the deviance***. While it is true that the use of drugs can cause organic impairment in some persons and thereby create antisocial acts, by far the majority of those performing antisocial acts while using drugs have ASPD. In the realm of criminal justice research on the relationship between drug use and crime, the findings have been clarified and solidified in that the criminal justice system has developed a firm stand.

"It is now clear that, '...research confirms the findings that crime precedes drug use and suggests that the relationship between drugs and crime is developmental rather than causal...' (Bureau of Justice Statistics, 1992b, p. 4). In short, drug use is a behavior that represents a developmental behavioral stage seen in those who are predisposed to the criminal lifestyle. In 1989 we wrote that, ...'criminals would be attracted to drug use... Drug use breeds criminal behavior and criminal behavior breeds drug use' (Robinson & Little, 1989). Data indicates that criminals are attracted to the use of drugs and that the use of drugs escalates the antisocial tendencies already present in offenders. Thus, the treatment of drug use is an important and ever-present issue in dealing with offenders since a reduction in substance use would reduce antisocial behavior (but not actually cease it). However, the basic underlying issue is the antisocial personality of offenders that attracts them to both crime and drugs" (Little & Robinson, 1994).

The summation that should be made from this discussion is not as complex as the evidence upon which it is based. Drug use among individuals with diagnosable ASPD and Conduct Disorder does not cause crime, but it can and does escalate their pre-existing criminal behavior. The use of drugs is one very commonly seen aspect of the

Quick Facts—

• The abuse of drugs is intimately tied to anti-social behavior and ASPD.

• Drug and alcohol use do not cause crime.

• ASPD and crime precede drug use.

• Criminals are attracted to drug use.

• Drug and alcohol use accelerate whatever antisocial tendencies are already present.

• ASPD and drug abuse may have the same underlying causes.

profile presented by antisocials. It is a behavior that reflects their risk-taking, sensation-seeking, and pleasure-seeking personality. As stated earlier, ASPD tends to develop early in life with a coinciding develop-ment of chemical abuse. The Office of Juvenile Justice and Delinquency Prevention's report on *Juvenile Offenders and Victims* (Snyder & Sickmund, 1995) states: "Researchers believe that delinquency and sub-stance abuse are caused by the same underlying factors, rather than one causing the other" (p. 63). That report goes on to say, "drug abuse does not cause the initiation of delinquent behavior, nor delinquent behavior the initiation of drug use. However, they may have the same root causes..." (p. 63).

Can anyone become an addict? In the field of chemical depen-dency treatment, it is common for people to state that "anyone can become an addict" and that "alcoholics come from all walks of life." Programs typically have preprinted brochures stating that chemical abuse causes all sorts of antisocial behaviors. From one perspective, that statement is partially true but it can also be quite misleading. **However, chemical abuse clearly accelerates whatever antisocial tendencies the abuser already has.** There is no research showing that chemical abuse turns non-antisocials into antisocials. Thus, when "normal" people abuse drugs (but do not cause organic damage to themselves), it would not be expected for them to perform antisocial acts to the extent that they are diagnosable with ASPD. Anyone *can* become an addict if they simply use drugs to the extent that they become physically dependent and experience withdrawal in the absence of the drug. And anyone *can* become an alcoholic if they drink frequently and in a sufficient quantity. *However, when criminals with ASPD use drugs or alcohol, **their criminal behavior accelerates and escalates**.* The text *The Mythology of Crime and Criminal Justice* (Kappeler, Blumberg, & Potter, 2000) relates, "there is little evidence that drugs cause crime...most addicts and abusers are involved in crime as a way of life; very few have a legitimate job; very few have enough education to make them marketable." With respect to drug and alcohol treatment programs, the important issues relate to effective treatment of abusers because the cessation of drug use will lower their criminal behavior. However, unless the underlying disorder of ASPD is addressed through an effective means, they will still perform criminal acts, and as research shows, will usually quickly relapse back to drug use.

ASPD in Chemical Dependency Treatment Programs

As previously mentioned, substance abuse programs operating outside of criminal justice often see the substance abuse diagnosis as overriding ASPD or any of its related personality disorders. The ASPD diagnosis, although usually suspected and clearly recognized, is "deferred" and is usually not revisited after treatment. The diagnosis is not revisited because such treatment is typically brief and patients are quickly released when the payment limits are reached, especially when a third party payer has established guidelines and timeframes. Thus, many of the "treated" clients are released and they frequently relapse—often quickly. The relapse is not usually seen as a "failure of the treatment program" instead, it is a failure placed on the client. In fact, favored program slogans and sayings, such as "this program will work for you if you work for it," reflect that it is the client and not the program that determines success and failure.

Chances are that the sentence in the last paragraph seems logical and reasonable to most readers. It does seem logical that the outcome of an individual's substance abuse treatment is determined by that person's engagement in the treatment. But with the increasing use of medical terminology in criminal justice treatment—e.g., Evidence-Based Treatment—an experimental medical example is appropriate.

If you took all the people who are diagnosed with pancreatic cancer in a given year and decided to treat them with a daily aspirin—or an apple, an orange, or anything else for that matter—and then followed their outcome, what would you conclude after 5 years? In general, you would find the following. Around 95% of the people would no longer be showing up for their daily treatment, but the 5% who were still taking the daily treatment would still be alive. Therefore, the aspirin works, right? If you work for it, it'll work for you, right? If you come in every day and take the aspirin, you'll make it for 5 years, but if you don't come in and take it, you'll die.

Hopefully the flaws in the above experiment are obvious. Looking at "successes" can be useful, but under some circumstances it can lead to very, very wrong conclusions.

Treatments for substance abuse and alcoholism are seldom blamed for their failures but they are given credit for their successes. However, if the treatment has focused on the drug use and not what is the primary underlying disorder—ASPD—then it can be surmised that the treatment is ineffective. Considerable evidence has been reported showing that a fairly large proportion of those entering virtually any type of treatment program for chemical dependency are diagnosable as having ASPD or a related Cluster B Personality Disorder. This implies that most substance abuse programs are treating antisocial individuals who have substance abuse problems; however, also implied is that the ASPD is seen as secondary (or even not important) in these programs. This fact may well account for the poor results most substance abuse programs have. A study conducted in Connecticut showed that 33% of cocaine *users* (not abusers) had ASPD regardless of whether they entered treatment or not (Rounsaville & Kleber, 1985). A study of cocaine *abusers* in New York City who entered outpatient treatment showed that 58% had Personality Disorders (Kleinman, Miller, Millman, Woody, Todd, Kemp, & Lipton, 1990). Diagnoses of New Orleans co-caine *users* entering a Veterans Hospital treatment program showed that 31% had Personality Disorders (Malow, West, Williams, & Sutker, 1989).

Substantial research has been done on the personality and diag-nosis of opiate and narcotic addicts entering treatment. Craig's (1993) survey reports that in all studies, about *67%* of those seeking treatment for narcotic use have ASPD or a related Personality Disorder. For ex-ample, in a study of narcotic abusers in a Veteran's Hospital program in Chicago (Craig, 1988), 72% had PDs. The afore mentioned New Or-leans study (Malow, *et al.*, 1989) found that 79% of opiate addicts had a PD. A 1992 study (Brooner, Schmidt, Felch, & Bigelow, 1992) found that 68% of inpatient and outpatient substance abusers who had in-jected drugs had ASPD. O'Boyle (1993) reported a 0.44 correlation between the multiple substance dependence and ASPD diagnoses in a group of 102 noncriminal substance abuse treatment patients who vol-unteered for the study. Thus, it is clear that many treatment programs that purport to treat substance abuse problems are treating clients who also have ASPD or another PD.

With regard to alcoholics, many treatment personnel have long considered alcoholism to have only a small overlap with ASPD and other personality disorders. Certainly, most treatment professionals rec-ognize that those persons who have frequent contact with the criminal justice system because of their alcoholism are antisocial. This finding is especially recognized in multiple DWI offenders. For example, a 10-year recidivism study of multiple DWI offenders showed that after ten years of release, 86.2 percent of nontreated offenders had been rear-rested (Little, Robinson, Burnette, & Swan, 1999). Research by the author's group has consistently shown that the vast majority of mul-tiple DUI/DWI offenders have ASPD.

Because of the nature and progression of alcoholism, many treat-ment programs outside of the criminal justice system have failed to consider the incidence of ASPD in their populations. One such study (Hesselbrock, Meyer, & Keener, 1985) conducted in Connecticut com-pared alcoholics in treatment from residential programs, a VA hospital-based program, and a University hospital program. This study showed

Quick Facts—

• 33 to 60 percent of cocaine abusers have ASPD or another personality disorder.

• 68 to 79 percent of opiate abusers have ASPD.

• 68 percent of intravenous drug users have ASPD.

• 49 percent of alcoholics have ASPD.

• Drug and alcohol use accelerate antisocial tendencies.

• ASPD and drug abuse may have the same underlying causes.

no major differences among client diagnoses in the three treatment sites. Results showed that 49% of the alcoholics were diagnosable with ASPD. Interestingly, this study did not utilize the use of alcohol and its attending problems with the diagnostic criteria. That is, disregarding all alcohol use and the problems associated with the alcohol use, 49% of the alcoholics in treatment programs were found to be antisocial. Others (Penick, *et al.*, 1984) have found similar results in alcoholics in treatment. Consistent with these findings, the text *Psychopharmacology: Basics for Counselors* (Little, 1997) describes three separate modern typologies that researchers have proposed to classify alcoholics. These typologies are similar and tend to divide alcoholics into two broad categories: those with ASPD and those that don't have ASPD. Each typology defines one type of alcoholic as having the characteristics of ASPD with an early onset of alcohol use coinciding with the antisocial behavior. The alcoholic types with strong ASPD characteristics are variously termed as *Type B, Type II,* or *Primary ASPD with Secondary Alcohol-*

ism. The other type of alcoholic (the non-ASPD) is apparently influenced more by environment and early-life learning.

Regarding the connection between ASPD and substance abuse, Freedman *et al.* (1975) stated, "Alcohol and drug abuse are seen with increased frequency among antisocials" (p. 1293). Page (1971) also cited excessive use of alcohol and drugs was common among ASPDs (p. 320), and virtually all studies on offenders have shown that 80% or more have substantial problems with chemical abuse (Gorski, 1993). Despite such findings, many providers of substance abuse treatment continue to insist that "noncriminal" abusers in treatment are very different from the criminal abusers. Farabee, Nelson, and Spence (1993) examined this claim by comparing a group of 136 criminal justice clients referred to outpatient substance abuse treatment to 40 self-referred clients to the same facility. On seven of eleven psychological variables, the two groups were virtually identical. Criminal justice clients, however, had higher decision-making scores (indicating better perceived efficacy in decision making). The noncriminal justice clients showed better ability to self-assess drug problems, had more desire for help, and had higher readiness for treatment.

Chapter 11

What Causes Antisocial Personality Disorder?

Two hundred years ago physicians and criminologists had no doubt that those with a criminal personality had been born that way. With the advent and influence of sociology and psychology in the 20th century, it was recognized that social conditions, environment, and upbringing played some role. Psychologists have viewed the development of ASPD as a socialization failure (Jenkins, 1960) stemming from environment (family and social background), heredity, and physiological differences in the sociopath. Studies have cited early maternal deprivation, separation from parents or family disintegration, rejection in the family life, and deviance on the part of parents or the primary caregivers as causative factors (see Freedman, *et al.*, 1976 for an overview of early research). But more modern research has returned to the genetics and physiology involved with ASPD and looked at how genetics interacts with environment. Today, there are literally thousands of studies published annually looking at some causal aspect of ASPD, Conduct Disorder, and other personality disorders.

Theories of ASPD are typically divided into biological (Hereditary), sociological, and psychological orientations (Ratliff, 1993). However, a comprehensive summary of research and findings is beyond the scope of this book. For the purposes of this text, only a brief overview of each shall be offered.

Biological & Genetic Theories

Biological theories have looked at genetic and hereditary consistencies in ASPDs, differences in physiological arousal levels between ASPDs and others, early-life organic brain damage, and differences in neurotransmitters, hormones, and other body chemicals. In general, there is data indicating that a multi-faceted hereditary influence is present, and a recent research focus on aggression and violence, sex crimes, and specific genes has occurred. This research goes far beyond the older research on twins and families. A good summary of the twin research is presented by Mason and Frick (1994) who reviewed 70 published studies on twins and adoptees and concluded, "heredity plays a significant role in the development of antisocial behavior... an average of approximately 50% of the variance in measures of antisocial behavior was accounted for by heredity. ... it is possible that our findings, which support the contention that there is an inherited predisposition to antisocial behavior, might even be an underestimate of the magnitude of the effects of heredity." A more recent review of the literature evaluating actual genes (Fishbein, 2000) concludes that genetic predispositions interact with environmental factors and influences to produce ASPD, alcoholism, and impulsive disorders.

In regards to Conduct Disorder, Phelps and McClintock (1994) reviewed the influence of heredity. They concluded that most studies show the range of hereditary influence on the development of Conduct Disorder between 24% to 90% with most studies averaging 45% to

---

Hereditary influences on ASPD and Conduct Disorder are probably responsible for 50 percent of the variance. These hereditary traits influence hormonal and brain chemical processes. NIDA research has now identified 89 separate genes influencing substance abuse and many may be related to ASPD.

55%. In addition, there are some significant differences in ASPDs and others in testosterone levels, serotonin levels, catecholamine, and cholesterol. For example, numerous studies point to high testosterone levels and violence, low cholesterol levels and violence, and low serotonin levels in brainstem areas of juvenile offenders. It is well known that ASPDs do not experience levels of anxiety and fear to the same extent as non-ASPDs, and data from the neurochemical and body chemistry studies have tended to confirm those findings (Benning, Patrick, & Iacona, 2005; Fung, *et al.*, 2005). A brief review of some of these studies follows.

Craig (2005) found that low levels of the enzyme Monoamine Oxidase A, which is genetically controlled, tends to create a susceptibility to the development of antisocial personality and aggression. A fairly large number of studies have focused on brain frontal lobe size and function in antisocials. The frontal lobe controls conscious decision-making and inhibitions. Mendez, *et al.* (2005) found that those with a right lobe dysfunction had a "diminished emotional concern for the consequences of their acts." Goethals, *et al.* (2005) found that individuals with Cluster B Personality Disorders tended to have lower metabolism of glucose and lower blood flow in the frontal cortex. Yang, *et al.* (2005) measured the actual volume of brain structures in psychopaths and nonpsychopaths using magnetic resonance imaging. Results showed that high scores on psychopathy were associated with a 22.3% reduction in the actual size of the frontal lobe. In an unusual study, Yang, *et al.* (2005b) used magnetic resonance imaging on pathological liars. The study concluded that the resulting 36-42% reduction that was found in prefrontal white/grey matter ratios implicated the prefrontal cortex as "an important component in the neural circuitry underlying lying... [in the] deceitful personality." Pridmore, Chanmers, & McArthur (2005) confirmed the observation that psychopaths have less volume in the prefrontal lobe. Barkataki, *et al.* (2006) found that antisocials evaluated with magnetic resonance imaging actually show lower total brain volume than nonantisocials. A more recent review (Narayan, *et al.*, 2007) has confirmed these findings.

In sum, research investigating genetic and anatomical differences between antisocials and others show clear differences in brain size and function, a variety of neurotransmitter differences, differences in reactivity, and clear genetic differences. The question that such research has not answered, at least definitively, is whether these differences were there at birth or whether some of them may have developed because of life experiences. However, most researchers believe that the genetic differences were present at birth. Viding, *et al.* (2005) for example, studied 3,686 twins and concluded that a strong genetic link to Conduct Disorder and antisocial behavior was present in 7-year-olds. Regarding the genetic evidence of ASPD and alcoholism, *Psychopharmacology* (Little, 1997) summarized the findings:

"A deluge of recent scientific reports have attempted to find specific genetic links to alcoholism, polysubstance abuse, and even personality disorders that are characterized by high levels of drug and alcohol use. Twin studies and the incidence of disorders across generations in families have led most researchers to believe that a genetic link must be present. Dopamine genes (including dopamine receptor genes and the dopamine reuptake transporter protein) have been found to be associated with both polydrug abuse and alcoholism (Blum, *et al.*, 1990; 1991; Smith, *et al.*, 1992). Some researchers consider the evidence overwhelming that alcoholism may be 30% to 50% or so genetically influenced with the remaining 70%-50% attributed to environmental and individual causes (Tarter, 1995), while other researchers remain skeptical (see Baron, 1993 for a brief review). Personality disorders in which those afflicted have high levels of alcoholism and/or substance abuse (e.g., Antisocial Personality Disorder) are also believed to be genetically based with up to 50% of the disorder attributed to genes (Thapar & McGuffin, 1993)."

Fishbein (2000) summarized 5 basic conclusions about the interaction of genetics and environment (Ch. 9, p. 34): 1. That numerous genetic and nongenetic variables produce the propensity for impulsive and aggressive behavior; 2. That several important genes have been identified with current technology and the information should be utilized and publicized; 3. There is definitive proof that several specific genes are involved and more are likely to be found; 4. That more carefully conducted gene/environment studies need to be conducted; and 5. That interventions exist that can improve these behavioral disorders.

Newer research techniques (NIDA Notes, 2008) have examined the actual genome sequences of DNA in drug dependent individuals. A NIDA sponsored study looked at specific genetic differences between 420 European American and 560 African American drug abusers and compared them to a control group of 680 ethnically-matched nonabusers. An astonishing 89 genes were found to be related to substance abuse. It is likely that future research will identify more such links and also match some of these to ASPD.

Sociological Theories

Sociologists have offered social learning theories, social control theories, subcultural theories, and various socioeconomic explanations for ASPD. Some support for all of the theories exists, but it is clear that the sociological explanations overlap some psychological theories and findings. Few sociologists have incorporated the genetic research into their theories. Modern sociologists have cited feelings of "socioeconomic segregation" as an explanation for how different crime rates exist in different locales. In addition, poor parenting techniques with inadequate discipline, early-life association with other poorly socialized children, and experiencing adult rejection in early life are all cited as factors. This environmental aspect, it is sometimes argued, explains why family studies show that ASPD and related disorders "run in families." One interesting finding that sociologists have perhaps uncovered and partially explained is why punishment has little or no effect on ASPDs. Termed "defiance theory," it shall be presented in the treatment section of this book.

Introductory psychology textbooks have long recognized the influence of upbringing, inadequate reasoning, and the lack of success treating those with ASPD. *Psychology: A Dynamic Science* (Schlesinger & Groves, 1976) stated: "Apparently, the presence of a sociopathic male model is an important factor in the antisocial male's development. The sociopath's thinking is aimed at justifying his antisocial behavior by blaming others. ... Because successful therapy depends upon the patient's anxiety and motivation to change, antisocial personalities are extremely difficult to treat" (p. 542).

Psychological Theories

In actuality, psychological literature and research has not un-covered a "criminal personality" as such. Rather, ASPDs and criminals tend to display a wide range of various personality characteristics to some degree or other. This range of characteristic variables can easily lead one to simplistically conclude that criminals and ASPDs are of all types. For example, intelligence and verbal skills vary greatly in ASPDs (as with non-ASPDs), as do other characteristics such as humor, looks, and social skills. However, if the core elements of ASPD (e.g., decep-tion, manipulation, lack of remorse) are kept in mind, criminal justice counselors can easily surmise that ASPD exists on a continuum of se-verity, and it can be present in individuals who seem to have vastly different personalities and skill levels.

Whether one accepts either the concept of psychopathy or the diagnosis of ASPD as they both apply to criminals, the idea of the crimi-nal personality is embedded in the very definitions and diagnostic cri-teria of both. *If there is a criminal personality, it is ASPD, and crimi-nal personality is embedded in the core of the disorder*—the attitudes and beliefs that lead to deception, taking advantage of others, and lack of remorse. As to how psychological theories account for ASPD, al-most all psychological theorists assert that heredity, environment, and early life experiences all play important roles as they interact with ge-netic predispositions. Research has uncovered several findings regard-ing early life influences. Early-life physical abuse, ineffective disci-pline, and poor relationships with parents are frequently found to be significant factors (Norden, Klein, Donaldson, Pepper, & Klein 1995). Smith and Thornberry (1995) researched the actual statistical effect of parental maltreatment on later antisocial behavior. They reported, "a history of maltreatment increases the probability of having an official (delinquency) record by .13 [i.e., 13%]." As mentioned at the end of the previous section on Biological & Genetic Theories, there is ad-equate evidence that heredity does play a role in the development of ASPD and that environmental influences (whether it be living condi-tions, parenting and family, or peers) interact profoundly with the pre-existing genetics. Many earlier explanations that can now be seen as overly-simplistic have created confusion and have added little to actual treatment success. One such simplistic explanation has been self-esteem. For decades efforts to instill high self-esteem in both school populations as well as with offenders and substance abusers have led to nothing but failed efforts.

It is interesting to note that violent criminals and those who display the extremes of ASPD tend to show high self-esteem, assertiveness, are very dogmatic, and believe they are socially desirable. In addition, they are high sensatio- seekers and thrill-seekers. In short, research on the ASPD client shows a core of similar pathology, with variation on the degree of pathology in each personality variable.

By far, the psychological theories of ASPD are the most accepted and popular among both treatment and criminal justice specialists. Those in criminal justice do not always agree, however, and many view ASPD as a nonpsychological behavioral disorder with its roots stemming from elsewhere. Those in juvenile justice are often at odds with all of the psychological, sociological, and biological theories. Gibbons' *Delinquent Behavior* (1970) stated:

"The psychogenic interpretation of delinquency has also enjoyed great popularity in the area of correctional treatment; therapeutic endeavors have often been predicated upon the assumption that the offender is a psychologically disturbed person who is in need of psychic tinkering of one kind or another. The treatment worker has often entertained an image of the juvenile offender as a defective electronic instrument which has been wired improperly or which has blown a tube. The therapy agent views his task as one of rewiring or repairing the person through some kind of psychiatric therapy....The popularity of psychogenic orientations to criminality and delinquency is certainly not due to any hard evidence....there is little convincing empirical support for the contention that delinquents are commonly plagued by emotional problems to which their deviant acts are a response....the majority of juvenile court referrals...do not appear to differ much in psychological well-being from nonoffenders." (p. 192)

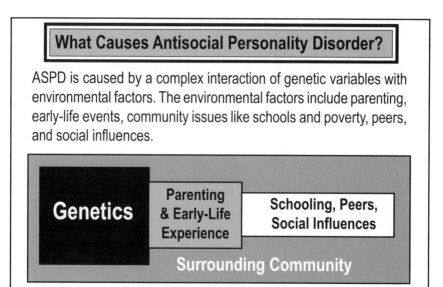

What Causes Antisocial Personality Disorder?

ASPD is caused by a complex interaction of genetic variables with environmental factors. The environmental factors include parenting, early-life events, community issues like schools and poverty, peers, and social influences.

Genetics

Parenting & Early-Life Experience

Schooling, Peers, Social Influences

Surrounding Community

In summary, what can be concluded about the causes of ASPD and related disorders is encapsulated in the title of a 2005 article in the journal *Behavioral Genetics*: Family dysfunction interacts with genes in the causation of antisocial symptoms (Button, *et al.*, 2005). The article concluded: "a risk genotype conferring susceptibility to family dysfunction is responsible for most of the variance in antisocial symptoms in childhood and adolescence."

If it's genetic, is it their fault? Can they really change?

When disorders are said to have some genetic cause, many people mistakenly believe that it can not be changed, and this provides the afflicted person with an excuse. If, for example, ASPD is a genetic predisposition that is exacerbated by the individual being born into an environment that encourages ASPD, then is the individual responsible and can it be changed? The answers are simple— yes, they are responsible. Yes, they can change.

One way of explaining this is found in another highly researched disorder that is on the increase in America—obesity. In 2000 the first two authors of this text coauthored a 424-page book on obesity, titled *It Can Break Your Heart* (Milnor, Little, & Robinson, 2000). Over 2000 recent medical studies were reviewed by the authors for the text, most of which focused on biological and genetic findings related to obesity. In sum, body mass (meaning one's actual weight as it is carried by the physical frame) is 70% due to heredity. With the Human Genome Project's completion in the mid-2000s and the mapping of three billion bits of genetic information that comprises human DNA, over 200 different genes have been directly linked to the development of obesity. A discussion of the specifics of the genetic influences is well beyond the scope of this book, but obesity (like ASPD) runs in families, and the genetic predispositions can be exacerbated and worsened by being in an environment where all the wrong behaviors are observed and encouraged. Anyone can theoretically become obese by routinely and consistently overeating. In a like manner, anyone can become an alcoholic or addict by routinely and consistently consuming these substances to excess. However, people who have the genetic predispositions to obesity will much more easily become obese because of biological processes that lead to a host of compounding problems. The simplistic solution that is given for obesity is to eat less, eat healthier, and be more active. In addition, there are medications and surgical procedures that can assist. In truth, with obesity, the simplistic solutions are the only ones that actually work. Eating less, eating healthier, and being more active do work and can be aided by medical interventions. People can not change their genetics, such as their height, their basic body build that is based on bone structure, and the way their hormones respond to certain foods such as sugar and fat. But the truth is that weight can be controlled—if the person is sufficiently motivated and has the knowledge required.

In a similar way, people with ASPD can change. Like too much food and the wrong food can worsen obesity, drugs and alcohol worsen ASPD behavior. The use of drugs and alcohol can be controlled, and this is something understood by the user just as the issue of food intake is understood by someone who is obese. Secondly, the core aspects of ASPD—the deception, thrill seeking, irresponsibility, impulsivity, manipulation, and associated attitudes—can be changed by application of appropriate treatment strategies. Treatment approaches that actually reduce the core aspects of ASPD do exist, but they are unfortunately not utilized to the extent that they are needed. The effective treatment of offenders and substance abusers is now where we go.

Chapter 12

Principles of Implementing Evidence-Based Practices in Criminal Justice Settings

Correctional treatment approaches faced a major turning point in the early 1970's with the publication of Robert Martinson's famed report in the journal *Public Interest* titled, "What works? Questions and answers about prison reform" (1974). Many interpreted Martinson's findings as implying that "nothing works" to reduce offender recidivism; however, in actuality, Martinson and his cohorts did find there were a few specialized programs that did show beneficial effects. In the 1970's and 80's many prison treatment specialists, including the present authors, attempted to distill the elements of programs that actually reduced reoffending and more carefully construct programs. Gradually, cognitive-behavioral programs were combined with therapeutic communities, educational and vocational programs, specialized court and probation programs, and truly effective programs were developed. These will be summarized in the next chapter. However, as the effective programs were developed and tested, the concept of criminogenic needs emerged, and efforts to better categorize offenders by risk and individual needs became another priority.

Testing & Assessments of Criminogenic Needs. At the same time that more effective programs were being developed, a new way of looking at offender populations emerged incorporating the concepts of evaluating specific risk areas and specific needs of individual offenders. While traditional standardized assessments and various tests were employed with offenders, a new category of assessment instruments were devised and tested during this time. One such test previously discussed was the PCL-R, which measures the construct of psychopathy.

However, that measure did not yield sufficient information on the emerging idea that an individual's criminogenic needs had to be identified. Various other tests that focus on substance abuse have also been utilized in criminal justice, but these too have limited applicability to criminogenic needs. In the 1990's the *Level of Service Inventory* (LSI-R) emerged in an attempt to measure offenders in 10 differing areas, which are essentially categories of needs specific to criminal populations (Andrews & Bonta, 1995). The LSI-R is a frequently employed assessment tool used today and has 54 items arranged into 10 general domains. The theoretical usefulness of the domains is that assessing the need and risk in each domain can lead to more informed decisions about what level of criminal justice supervision is necessary (or ideal) for each offender and what specific programs or interventions are appropriate. Like the other assessment tools, the LSI-R requires a structured interview but also requires supporting documentation from family, employers, drug testing, and other sources. The criminogenic need domains covered by the LSI-R include education/employment, finances, relationships, housing, recreational activities, friends, alcohol & substance use, mental health, and attitudes—as well as overall criminal history. A total risk score is used to attempt to predict possible recidivism, and scores on the various domains are used to make supervision and program assignments. In general, research supports the LSI-R as statistically valid and reliable, but the limitations are important to understand. especially since the tool is so widely utilized. One limitation is the ability of the test to predict future recidivism. This has notably failed to occur in several studies and also failed in different criminal justice settings. Secondly, but just as important as the first limitation, is the finding that the usefulness of the LSI-R as a classification tool has to be researched and validated within each particular type of program and institution dealing with the various types of offender populations (Flores, *et al.*, 2006).

One research example of the limitations of the LSI-R was found in a large sample of offenders in Pennsylvania (Austin, *et al.*, 2003) who were released on parole. The study, conducted on over 1,000 offenders in several phases, found that only 18 of the LSI-R's 54 items were statistically reliable to the degree where consistency between raters (the trained professionals administering the tests) could be considered to be reliable. In addition, there was "substantial disagreement between two interviewers regarding the risk level." A second phase of the study was able to raise the reliability of the 54 items from only 18 to a more respectable 34. The validity of the LSI-R was measured by the one-year recidivism rate of the group. Half of the parolees had recidivated within that period. A statistical analysis showed that only 8 of the 54 items of the LSI-R were significantly correlated to recidivism with most of these key items reflecting prior drug usage and criminal history. The study concluded that the LSI-R has "problematic reliability" as it pertained to offenders in Pennsylvania institutions and recommended that it not be used to assess risk during a parole interview. With respect to the validity of the instrument—its ability to predict one-year recidivism—the authors recommended that the few items that do correlate to recidivism (8 of 54) could be used to assess risk to some degree or that a revised version of the instrument might be tried.

The LSI-R, PCL-R, and various other assessment tools remain in widespread use and are constantly being researched. The potential usefulness of such assessment tools is extremely important. However, the utilization of a single valid and reliable testing instrument remains elusive. In addition, many other tests, such as the COMPAS (Brennan *et. al.*, 2009), are used to assign offenders to programs based on needs.

Evidence-Based Practices Emerge
Leading to Treatment Principles

With the development of more effective programs, research was conducted which identified specific elements that were consistently found in these programs. These key factors eventually became a framework for more effective correctional practices. Latessa (2000) summarized the factors into four broad treatment principles: 1. Interventions should target higher risk offenders (known as the Risk Principle); 2. Interventions should target the actual needs of criminals (known as the Criminogenic Need Principle); 3. Offenders, specific programs, and staff should be matched (known as the Responsivity Principle); and 4. Treatment should be behavioral in nature (known as the Treatment Principle). In addition, within the realm of criminal treatment in a world with limited resources and limited time, the treatments that are utilized with offenders should show actual effectiveness in reducing recidivism. Programs and approaches that have reliable and valid data supporting their actual effectiveness came to be known as *Evidence-Based Practices*, which is adapted terminology from medical research. In short, to receive funding many programs treating offender populations and substance abusers are now required to employ a treatment approach that is recognized as *Evidence-Based*. Chapter 14 describes programs and treatment approaches that have been recognized as Evidence-Based.

The National Institute of Corrections (2004) issued a more detailed set of guidelines which are organized as a set of principles on how to implement evidence-based practices in accordance with currently accepted knowledge. Eight principles were outlined in their report; however, it is important to note that not all of these have reached the status of universal recognition or actual implementation.

The Eight Principles of Utilizing Evidence-Based Practices

1. Assess Needs & Risks. This principle assumes that a valid and reliable set of measures exists to assess offenders on their specific needs and actual risks. Some issues, such as educational needs, substance abuse treatment needs, and vocational needs can be reliably ascertained in intake assessments and through drug testing; however, the ability to predict future violence and recidivism remains weak. Testing instruments like the PCL-R , the LSI-R, COMPAS, sensation seeking scales, and MMPI are still widely utilized in the criminal justice system, yet, as previously mentioned, a genuinely valid and reliable measure applicable to all offenders has not been identified.

2. Enhance Intrinsic Motivation. In the early 2000's motivational interviewing emerged as a method utilized to assess an offender's desire to change (basically by assessing their *readiness to change* on a scale) and to increase the individual's intrinsic motivation to change. Results from a variety of studies showed that the technique (a nonjudgmental process of eliciting information and providing feedback) enhanced the degree to which offenders engaged in treatment, leading to increased treatment effectiveness as evidenced by several studies evaluating 3-6-month outcomes. The effectiveness of the method, which

> # The Eight Principles of Evidence-Based Practices
>
> 1. Assess Needs & Risks
> 2. Enhance Intrinsic Motivation
> 3. Target Interventions
> 4. Utilize Cognitive-Behavioral Method for Skills
> 5. Use Positive Reinforcement
> 6. Provide Community Support
> 7. Measure Outcomes
> 8. Provide Feedback to Offenders & Staff

typically is performed in 2 to 4 brief sessions prior to treatment, is more pronounced in short-term evaluations but it dissipates somewhat as the time frame used to evaluate recidivism is increased. A more recent followup study (Adamson & Sellman, 2008) found that after 5 years the beneficial treatment effect of motivational interviewing had completely disappeared.

3. Target Interventions. Five different items comprise the principle of targeting interventions. These are 1) *Risk Principle*: prioritize supervision and treatment resources to higher risk offenders; 2. *Need Principle*: assess offenders' criminogenic needs focusing on dynamic (changeable) needs. These include antisocial beliefs and attitudes, self-control and impulsivity, peer influence, substance abuse, educational level, and vocational skills; 3. *Responsivity Principle*: matching treatment approaches to offender characteristics such as cultural and gender differences, specifically utilizing proven-effective cognitive-behavioral approaches; 4. *Dosage Principle*: providing sufficient treatment and supervision rather than brief services. It is generally accepted that higher risk offenders should engage in full-time programming for 3-9 months; and 5. *Treatment Principle*: Cognitive-behavioral treatment should be utilized with most offenders at all levels of supervision, with the possible exception of some low-risk offenders on diversion.

4. Skill Training. This principle is another specifying that cognitive-behavioral programs—especially those proven to reduce recidivism—should be utilized with offenders by trained staff. The use of an *Evidence-Based Program* is necessary.

5. Positive Reinforcement. Some form of external rewards to enhance extrinsic motivation must be used in programs with offenders. It is recommended that the ratio be four reinforcements to each negative reinforcement (or punishment). Positive reinforcement can be of a wide range of verbal and actual rewards. Some programs provide vouchers and small rewards such as personal items or food.

6. Provide On-Going Community Support. Aftercare programs and programs that engage family and other significant people in an offender's treatment are more effective over the lon- term.

7. Measure Outcomes. These include routine recidivism studies to assess the effectiveness of programs. In addition, outcomes that measure staff performance within programs are necessary.

8. Provide Feedback. Offenders should be given feedback on their progress and changes and feedback should also be given to staff on the measures that assess the program's effectiveness and outcomes.

Program Integrity. In a more recent text entitled *What Works in Corrections* (MacKenzie, 2006), the issue of program integrity is stressed. In general, the concept of *program integrity* encapsulates the entire realm of effective treatment principles into a single sentence: "A program has integrity if it incorporates such things as a clearly identified rationale consistent with the human service theoretical literature, qualified and trained staff to deliver the program, treatment methods shown to be effective, and a consistent protocol" (p. 55). MacKenzie analyzes the various eight principles listed above giving a candid set of observations. In her discussion of the Need Principle (that individual needs and risks should be targeted), the point is made that some approaches fail to target genuine criminogenic needs. "One good example of a characteristic not necessarily related to criminal activity is self-concept or self-esteem. Self-esteem is unrelated or only weakly related to recidivism... Offenders and juvenile delinquents can and do have high self-esteem" (p. 59). As to focusing treatment on the highest risk offenders, MacKenzie stresses that while the principle is generally accepted in treatment circles, the results have been mixed. In addition, research shows that educational level and vocational achievement were also less important risk factors. The most critical needs for criminal offenders are antisocial personality with the associated beliefs and attitudes. As to the issue of treatment modality, MacKenzie has found that casework, individual counseling, and self-reflective and insight-oriented approaches are ineffective.

Quick Facts—

• A truly reliable and valid assessment instrument has yet to be devised.

• The PCL-R and LSI-R are the two most frequently used screening and assessment tools, with some effectiveness shown in some places.

• The Principles of Effective Treatment are guidelines that should be followed when establishing correctional programming.

• Cognitive-behavioral programming of a sufficient duration is state-of-the-art in corrections today.

• A program that has integrity is one that has a clearly identified rationale; uses an effective, evidence-based method; uses competent and trained staff; and has a consistent protocol.

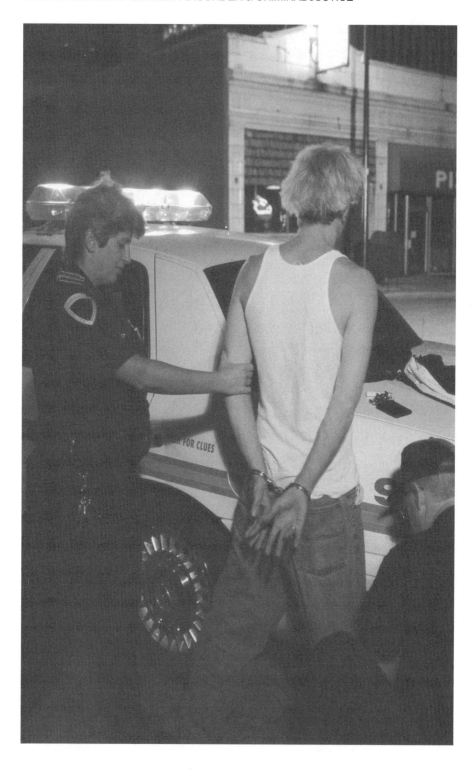

Chapter 13

Ineffective Treatment of ASPD and Substance Abuse: What Doesn't Work

Prior to the mid-1980's, few professionals treating criminals and/or those with ASPD claimed any marked degree of success (Martinson, 1979). Textbooks in corrections, criminal justice, and clinical psychology often recommended that offenders be incapacitated and held accountable for their actions and then "waited out." This was in recognition that a fairly large proportion of ASPDs simply "slow down" when they reach their late 30s and early 40s. Abusers and offenders at these ages often state, "I'm getting too old for this," or "I just can't do as much as I used to." Page's text (1971) remarked on how ASPDs' antisocial behavior progresses during adolescence, peaks in their 20s, and then tends to gradually taper off. ASPD invariably begins before the age of 15; however, boys typically show symptoms before age 12. Its height occurs in late adolescence and early adulthood. By the time the antisocial is in his mid-40s, about 40% have shown substantial improvement.

The improvement of ASPD with age is clearly a function of age rather than therapeutic intervention. Page (1971) stated: "After the age of thirty, about a third of these patients show a moderation of overt antisocial behavior, but interpersonal relations continue to be marked by irritability and hostility ... The decline in antisocial behavior appears to be mainly a function of aging" (p. 320).

ASPD has been considered untreatable by many professionals who recommend that institutions incapacitate the offender until they age and become less severe and less obvious sociopaths. The 1954 text, *An Introduction To Clinical Psychology* (Pennington & Berg) stated:

"...for years these expressive personalities have been considered untreatable by many..." (p. 441). "The fact that the pure psychopath has been considered an amoral person devoid of conscience and all other adjudged desirable attributes has led many to conclude, without therapeutic effort, that he is 'hopeless'" (p. 443). Page (1971) is perhaps typical in citing the lack of effective treatment for the ASPD during the decades of the 1970's and 80's.

"The effectiveness of psychotherapy is influenced by personal distress on the part of the patient, a strong desire to change, the establishment of a warm, trusting relationship with the therapist, and mutual expectation of beneficial results. Since the sociopath sees nothing wrong with his behavior, which he finds rewarding, at least in the short run, he has no incentive to change and no interest in establishing an emotional relationship with the therapist, of which he is incapable in any case. The therapist, for his part, has been conditioned by his training and experience to regard sociopathy as incurable" (p. 321).

Literature reviews and studies tend to reveal that most treatments applied to clients with ASPD have low success rates if they are at all successful. For example, Woody, McClellan, Luborsky, & O'Brien (1985) studied treating depression, opiate addiction, and ASPDs with some groups having overlapping diagnoses. They stated: "Antisocial personality disorder alone is a negative predictor of psychotherapy outcome." In short, the current evidence clearly shows that traditional substance abuse programming either does not work to change the antisocial abuser or actually makes them worse.

Summary of Outcome Research—What Doesn't Work—Or Doesn't Work Too Well

Many chemical dependency treatment personnel and corrections staff are unfamiliar with the vast outcome literature on treating drug- and alcohol-abusing offenders. Palmer's (1993) large meta-analysis on recidivism outcome studies on offenders indicated that the following approaches either do not work to reduce recidivism or actually increase it: confrontive (scared straight) approaches, vocational training, employment programs, individual counseling that is non-behavioral in nature, psychotherapy, diversion, physical challenge, and basic education programs. In 1994, the Center for the Study and Prevention of Violence published an extensive report citing the effectiveness of various approaches for juvenile offenders (Tolan & Guerra, 1994). Among the ineffective approaches addressed in this report are psychotherapy, casework, guided group interactions, and scare programs.

MacKenzie's (2006) meta-analyses conducted on the vast body of literature covered virtually every approach typically used with offenders. Her summaries of the outcomes of the reviews are as follows for selected approaches:

Academic Education. Most institutions provide some form of educational programs such as GED classes, basic literacy, and occasionally college level classes. It is generally accepted that such programs are necessary and could be seen as an obligation. That is, basic education should be provided whether or not it reduces recidivism. Despite the pervasiveness of educational programming, the research that has been done evaluating these programs is of low quality and highly limited. MacKenzie cites several large reviews that state outright that educational programs in and of themselves do not reduce recidivism. However, in recent years educational programs have also utilized "life skills" in their curriculum, sometimes employing evidence-based cognitive-behavioral treatment programs. Results from these more recently developed educational programs shows that offender recidivism is reduced somewhat. Whether it is the education itself or the added components that are responsible for the recidivism reduction has not been partialed out by the research; however, it is likely that the educational component, in and of itself is limited in effectiveness.

Vocational Programs & Work Programs. Unemployment has long been related to criminal activity, and specific vocational programs have been developed and utilized. Results from many studies show that specific vocational training can reduce recidivism moderately but that prison industries and other prison work programs do not. Unfortunately, out of necessity created by limited resources, vocational programs tend to offer only a few selected opportunities. For example, some programs train only cooks while others are focused on electronics or engine repair. These can be useful, but are only appropriate for a small percentage of offenders.

Sex Offender Treatment. In the 1990's the evidence related to treatments for sex offenders showed that there was "no convincing evidence that treatment reduces future sex offending" (p. 149). However, with the addition of cognitive-behavioral programming that specifically targeted sex offending issues, MacKenzie concluded that some sex offender programs do, in fact, reduce future recidivism. The MRT-based sex offender relapse prevention method, *Making Changes For Good* (Little & Robinson, 1998) is an example of a cognitive-behavioral model.

Juvenile Justice Programs. For some years, the *Scared Straight* type of program was popular; however, it was quickly realized that the approach did little to reduce future recidivism. In fact, "Not only are Scared Straight programs not effective, they appear to have a detrimental effect" (p. 171). MacKenzie also found that juvenile supervision programs were not effective, nor were wilderness programs or employment programs.

Boot Camps. Boot camps have been extensively used with both juveniles and adults. The results of many studies show clearly that boot camps are not effective at reducing recidivism. The exceptions may be boot camps that utilize some cognitive-behavioral approaches in addition to the discipline-oriented boot camp environment. One such example was a Tennessee based juvenile boot camp that was operated as a therapeutic community (Burnette, *et al.*, 2004). Boot camps are however, politically and institutionally seen as showcases and mainly useful as a means to impress public attitudes and perceptions. The use of a cognitive-behavioral component is essential in all such programs.

Intensive Supervision Programs. Parole and probation have extensively utilized electronic monitoring and highly structured and frequent monitoring programs on offenders. "A large body of research ... consistently shows the failure of ISP and EM programs to lower recidivism" (p. 322).

The present authors' extensive reviews and writings on outcome literature on treating substance abusers with ASPD is in line with MacKenzie's findings and also reveals the following:

1. No studies exist in the treatment outcome literature demonstrating that any educational programs have ever reduced subsequent antisocial behaviors by convicted drunk drivers (Foon, 1988). Some cognitive-behavioral programs do however reduce subsequent offending by treated DUI offenders.

2. No studies exist in the treatment outcome literature demonstrating that any traditional counseling approaches or 12-Step programs have reduced antisocial behaviors by convicted drunk drivers during the five years after their treatment (Eliny & Rush, 1992; Foon, 1988).

3. No studies exist in the treatment outcome literature showing that any form of drug education (by itself) or 12-Step (AA) based programs reduce the subsequent antisocial behavior of drug offenders (Gendreau & Ross, 1987; Lipton, Falkin, & Wexler, 1990; Little, Robinson, & Burnette, 1992). In fact, AA itself is not touted as treatment; it is a self-help support group.

4. No studies exist in the treatment outcome literature showing that traditional client-centered or psychodynamic therapies have reduced antisocial behavior by any offender groups (Gendreau & Ross, 1987; Lipton, Falkin, & Wexler, 1990; Little, Robinson, & Burnette, 1992).

5. About half of the outcome studies published in treatment literature on educational, traditional counseling, and 12-Step programs applied to alcohol or substance abusing offenders show that treated offenders fare worse than nontreated offenders (Eliny &Rush, 1992; Foon, 1988; Gendreau & Ross, 1987; Lipton, Falkin, & Wexler, 1990; Little, Robinson, & Burnette, 1992).

6. Programs and approaches that do work on ASPD substance-abusing clients share certain commonality and consistencies in procedures and philosophy. Therapeutic community and cognitive-behavioral interventions have shown significant declines in antisocial behavior and substance use by treated offenders (Bureau of Justice Statistics, 1992b; Little, Robinson, & Burnette, 1993; Little & Robinson,1989; Little & Robinson, 1994).

Over the years, many texts have cautioned against using inappropriate treatment methodologies with offenders and those with ASPD. Freedman, *et al.* (1976) stated, "...the usefulness of outpatient psychotherapy along traditional lines for the offender is highly questionable..." Regarding the applicability and limitations of Rogerian interventions (person-centered or client-centered therapy), Corsini's once widely-used textbook, *Current Psychotherapies* (1973) cautioned: "The client-centered approach is theoretically applicable to any relationship where the persons want to understand each other and want to be understood; where the persons are willing to reveal themselves to some degree; and where the persons wish to enhance their own growth" (p. 153).

Within the limitations of person-centered counseling lies its weakness with ASPD. First, ASPDs do not necessarily want to be understood. Secondly, ASPDs do not wish to open up or reveal themselves; by their nature they are deceptive. Third, ASPDs do not want to grow for the simple reason that they do not consider themselves to be the problem.

Pennington and Berg's 1954 textbook, *An Introduction To Clinical Psychology,* stated the most appropriate use of Rogerian therapy:

"Its most obvious area of applicability has been with college students" (p. 528). This text goes on to say, "The client-centered method has wide application to the treatment of the emotional problems of normal persons..." (p. 548).

Modern counseling texts typically state the limitations of a particular theory in a summary section. With client-centered therapy, invariably it is stated that the technique has limited usefulness on antisocial clients. Despite this limitation, the tenets of client-centered therapy are often cited by textbooks used in the training of substance abuse counselors as being desirable, necessary, and effective counseling techniques. For example, the still commonly-used text *Essentials of Chemical Dependency Counseling* (Lawson, Ellis, & Rivers, 1984) has large sections devoted to restating what the clients say, reflecting back their feelings and content, developing empathy with clients, showing acceptance and reassurance of clients, and content clarification. These are, of course, the main essentials of client-centered therapy. The same text cites no outcome data whatsoever indicating that the technique actually reduces substance abuse—only that they should be used. The graduate text *Theories and Strategies In Counseling and Psychotherapy* (Gilliland, James, & Bowman, 1994) cautions that Rogerian counseling is adequate for "healthy" clients but is problematic with more disturbed clients. It recommends that the approach can be used effectively when dealing with cultural issues, coping with disabilities, and bereavement. The text cautions against using the method when clients need goal-directedness, reinforcement, short-term concrete results, and structured guidance—or when dealing with clients who have problems with mores and lifestyles. To summarize, client-centered counseling is usually an inappropriate approach with offenders when recidivism reduction is the goal.

Chapter 14

Evidence-Based Programs for Offenders & Substance Abusers: What Works to Reduce Recidivism

There are literally hundreds of treatment programs and treatment approaches in existence with many of them advertised as "evidence-based." Some programs and approaches simply self-proclaim that they are evidence-based. In other cases, some promotional program materials will refer to *another* evidence-based accredited program and state it is "identical to," "similar to," "equivalent to," or "the same as" another evidence-based program—without offering any evidence whatsoever. Programs claim they "work," "reduce recidivism," or are "effective" often without a shred of evidence or sometimes citing outcome data from some other program. For example, promotional literature might state that "it is proven that cognitive-behavioral treatment lowers recidivism by 30%, and our program is cognitive-behavioral." Slickly produced full-color promotional catalogs will show program materials with the term "evidence-based" on every page and with every workbook, without citing a single reference. Until very recent times, correctional programs and drug treatment have actually had what often seems to be a near absence of ethics as it pertains to claimed results and program effects, and in many instances this persists to the present. With such a high recidivism rate known to be present in the criminal justice system, it is no wonder that treatment professionals are accorded little to no credibility by other criminal justice professionals. When choosing an evidence-based program, professionals should ask for outcome research—but not research on *other* programs—research on the specific program being marketed.

In addition, outcome research studies in the offender and substance abuse treatment fields are known to have been conducted with major biases designed to make programs "look good." One frequently found example of such research is when programs compare their successes to their failures. What this means in the simplest of terms is that *many programs actually tout their effectiveness by comparing people who successfully complete their program to people who enter their program and are rearrested, relapse, or simply disappear.* In essence, what they are oddly claiming is that the people who are successful in their program are more successful than the people who are unsuccessful in their program. Of course, that's not the way the study is described, but in essence that is what is done. The common way this occurs is when a program compares its dropouts to those who complete their treatment. Treatment completers are always "more successful" than dropouts because many dropouts do so when they relapse to drug use, are rearrested, abscond, or go into "hiding." In general, the highest-risk clients will relapse sooner and in greater numbers than low-risk clients. Thus, high-risk clients become dropouts while low-risk clients become completers. A good example of this type of study was mentioned in Chapter 10: "If you took all the people who are diagnosed with pancreatic cancer in a given year and decided to treat them with a daily aspirin—or anything else for that matter—and then followed their outcome, what would you conclude after 5 years? In general, what you would find is the following. Around 95% of the people would no longer be showing up for their daily treatment, but the 5% who were still taking the daily treatment would still be alive. Therefore, the aspirin works, right?"

In truth, this is precisely what many programs do. They claim success because those who completed their programs are more successful than those who dropped out or were terminated. It is seldom determined if there is some sort of important difference between the completers and those who dropped out. With respect to the pancreatic cancer study, there was an important difference between those who dropped out and those who completed. The dropouts probably all died or became so incapacitated that they could no longer show up. Do we blame the patients who die during cancer treatment for their failure to live and complete the treatment? The answer is *no*; we come to the conclusion that the treatment did not work for those patients. But in substance abuse treatment, we almost always blame the patient. A negative or undesirable outcome (relapse) in substance abuse treatment is typically blamed on the client. The treatment's overall effectiveness is seldom questioned. It is assumed by these programs that the program works, if the client will stay sober, drug-free, and crime-free. Of course, those are the aims of the program. So why do they fail to acknowledge the program's failures? The answer is that such programs are rarely as effective as they claim. A program's effectiveness must be determined by all of its participants, not just those who are "successful."

The emerging idea of "Evidence-Based" programs recognizes that some treatment approaches are better than others and that if too many people fail to complete a program, perhaps the program's structure or approach is actually ineffective. Returning a moment to the pancreatic cancer treatment study, could it be that the aspirin might have helped the 5% who lived? The only way to tell is to determine how many people who are diagnosed with pancreatic cancer will survive after 5 years with a daily aspirin as opposed to those who do not get an aspirin. A good comparison group (a control group) is needed.

What that means is that outcome research on various programs' effectiveness has different degrees of usefulness and different degrees of quality. Some outcome studies are better than others, and in general the more research that has been done the better. The emerging emphasis on *Evidence-Based Programs* recognizes that only certain kinds of research will lead to genuine knowledge on precisely what a given program's effects actually are. Obviously, everyone who enters a given treatment program should be included and there should always be an appropriate nontreated comparison group. All outcome research that *only* compares treatment completers with treatment dropouts should be examined carefully while remembering that the conclusions of such research are suspect. Ideally individuals in both the comparison group and the treated group should be randomly placed into the two groups from a pool of individuals who have been approved for the treatment. In reality, such random selection—which constitutes a true experiment— is rare and difficult to accomplish in treatment. However, there are other ways to organize such a study wherein the treated and untreated comparison groups can be essentially the same, with no differences between the groups that would lead to a bias in the results. Such research is called *quasi-experimental*. The evaluation of programs for inclusion in recognized "Evidence-Based Program" lists utilize measures that assess the quality of the research design as well as the consistency of outcomes, the outcomes of the program at various sites (replications), and the ability of the program to be duplicated (the degree to which a program can be set up and operated elsewhere with the same general results obtained).

There are a host of agencies, organizations, state departments, and colleges that have published lists of what they consider to be *Evidence-Based Programs and Practices*. While these are generally useful, they also create a great deal of confusion because nearly every program and approach in existence can be listed by someone—somewhere—as *Evidence-Based*. There are some organizations and agencies that established an Evidence-Based list in order to include one of more of their *own* programs. Two agencies of the U.S. Federal Government are, however, considered to be the highest level of "Evidence-Based" recognition. The National Institute on Drug Abuse (**NIDA**) and the Substance Abuse & Mental Health Services Administration (**SAMHSA**) both officially recognize *Evidence-Based Programs and Practices*. Those are our recommended sources for information on choosing programming. Both lists will be reviewed here, with SAMHSA's NREPP program first.

SAMHSA's National Registry of Evidence-Based Programs and Practices (NREPP)

SAMHSA's National Registry of Evidence-Based Programs and Practices (NREPP) is available as a searchable online database and is updated as programs are added to their registry (www.nrepp.samhsa.gov/about-evidence.asp). On its website, SAMHSA relates: "In the health care field, evidence-based practice (or practices), also called EBP or EBPs, generally refers to approaches to prevention or treatment that are validated by some form of documented scientific evidence."

"NREPP originated in 1997 in SAMHSA's Center for Substance Abuse Prevention (CSAP) as part of their Model Programs Initiative. ... More than 1100 programs were reviewed and more than 150 were designated as Model, Effective, or Promising Programs under this system. In 2004, SAMHSA started the process of expanding this system to include interventions in mental health prevention and treatment. ... Launched in March 2007, SAMHSA's new registry [with its online searchable database] is designed to serve as a more comprehensive and interactive source of information than the previous system. ... In addition, NREPP now evaluates and reports on a new dimension called Readiness for Dissemination, a concept not part of earlier NREPP reviews."

The minimum requirements for NREPP designation include at least one statistically significant outcome study with at least one study using an experimental or quasi-experimental design. The research must have been published in a peer-reviewed journal or other recognized publication or comprehensive evaluation report. Materials for program implementation and quality assurance must be available for dissemination and review. The review process is rigorous with most NREPP programs having multiple publications showing success. However, even SAMHSA cautions those selecting programs to make their own judgments and evaluations about programming.

As of February 2010, NREPP had validated and listed 151 interventions with 26 of these programs in general criminal justice. A total of 6 NREPP programs are specifically validated in corrections. Most of these are substance abuse treatment programs with a few also employed in general offender treatment (or *offender rehabilitation* as some people might describe it). Programs are validated separately for adults and juveniles as well as for a host of other population specific characteristics (e.g., gender, mental health). As the database adds programs that are approved by the review process, readers are encouraged to go to the SAMHSA database for updates. A summary of the 6 NREPP programs listed in corrections follows with a few of the most relevant criminal justice programs also described. One program discussed in this section, ***Moral Reconation Therapy (MRT®),*** is a widely-implemented, highly researched, major cognitive-behavioral program used in virtually all levels of offender treatment and drug treatment, as well as for both juveniles and adults. MRT is more thoroughly described in the next chapter and was developed by the present authors. Quotes listed with the following programs are from the NREPP website.

Brief Strategic Family Therapy. This program is aimed at adolescents to prevent and treat behavioral problems.

CASASTART. This is a community-based school-centered substance abuse and violence prevention program for adolescents.

Forever Free. This is a program aimed at incarcerated "women who abuse drugs." The program is comprised of individual counseling, specialized workshops and seminars, 12-Step programs, urine screens, and parole planning.

Friends Care. This is a highly specialized support program for "probationers and parolees exiting mandated outpatient substance abuse treatment. The aftercare program is designed to maintain and extend the gains of court-ordered outpatient treatment..."

Living in Balance. This is a relapse prevention program consisting of workbook-based sessions delivered in 12 core group meetings with 21 supplemental sessions.

Methadone Maintenance. This is a medication used as a treatment for narcotic (primarily heroin) addiction. It is discussed in more detail in the NIDA section that follows.

Modified Therapeutic Community for Persons With Co-Occurring Disorders. A more detailed discussion of therapeutic communities (TC) can be found in the next chapter. This specific modified TC is a 12 to 18-month residential program for individuals with a diagnosed substance abuse disorder who also have a co-occurring mental disorder.

Moral Reconation Therapy ®. Moral Reconation Therapy, or MRT®, was first implemented within a prison-based substance abuse TC program in 1985 by the authors of this text. Over 100 outcome studies on MRT have been published. As opposed to the age limits and treatment location specificity of the other described NREPP programs, MRT was designed to be a treatment approach that could be utilized with adults or juveniles within any facility or program, and at any level of supervision—be it parole, probation, jails, prisons, treatment centers, or even schools. MRT is a cognitive-behavioral program conducted in ongoing groups where new clients can enter at any time and work at individualized paces. MRT focuses on enhancing moral reasoning, decision-making skills, and it directly addresses criminal thinking and criminal behavior, including substance abuse and antisocial behavior. More details on MRT can be found in following chapters.

Multidimensional Family Therapy. This is a comprehensive family-based outpatient or partial hospitalization program for adolescents and juveniles with substance abuse problems who may or may not have a co-occurring mental disorder.

Multidimensional Family Therapy for Juvenile Offenders. This program "addresses the multidimensional nature of behavior problems in troubled youth. Treatment focuses on those factors in each youth's social network that are contributing to his or her antisocial behavior."

Parenting with Love and Limits. This is a combination of group and family therapy for children and adolescents (ages 10-18) with severe emotional and behavioral problems.

Phoenix Academy. This therapeutic community (TC) model is specialized for adolescents. The TC model is discussed in more detail later.

Second Step. This classroom-based program is used on children ages 4 to 14 and focuses on social skills to reduce impulsive and aggressive behavior.

Strengthening Families Programs. Two separate models are in this program, both focusing on family skills to increase resilience in children and adolescence, as well as to reduce risk factors.

TCU Mapping-Enhanced Counseling. This Texas Christian University program is a decision-making and communication technique designed to improve counselor and client interactions through the use of graphic visualization tools.

NIDA's Evidence-Based Approaches to Drug Addiction Treatment

NIDA (2009) has sponsored research and published a list of recommended pharmacotherapies titled *Principles of Drug Addiction Treatment: A Research Based Guide*. In reality, most of NIDA's recommendations are seldom followed in jails and prisons for reasons that are obvious to those working in the system. The use of medications to treat substance abuse is considered by many to often be impractical within criminal justice institutions. However, some American drug courts, probation and parole settings, and substance abuse treatment programs employ NIDA's evidence-based medication recommendations. NIDA recommends that all medication therapies be combined with some behavioral therapies. NIDA's evidence-based programs are as follows:

Methadone Maintenance for Opiate Addiction. Methadone is a substitute for opiate-related narcotics (such as heroin). The medication is administered by specially registered physicians and in specialized methadone maintenance clinics. Methadone blocks withdrawal symptoms, decreases craving, and blocks the effects of illegal opiates. In general, the medication is given in conjunction with individual and group counseling as well as other support services.

Buprenorphine for Opiate Addiction. Buprenorphine is similar to methadone but has a lower risk of overdose. The trade name versions of the drug are as Subutex® or Suboxone®. Physicians with a specialized accreditation can prescribe these medicines in an outpatient office setting.

Naltrexone for Opiate Addiction and Alcohol Addiction. Naltrexone is an opiate blocker with few side effects. That is, those who take naltrexone cannot feel the effects of an opiate narcotic even if they take an illegal drug such as heroin. Naltrexone is also useful with alcohol addiction as it blocks cravings for alcohol and the rewarding effects of ingesting alcohol. Naltrexone reduces relapse during the first three months but is less effective in maintaining long-term abstinence.

Acamprosate for Alcohol Addiction Withdrawal. Acamprosate (Campral®) is effective in reducing some of the symptoms of alcohol withdrawal which include anxiety and insomnia, restlessness, and malaise.

Disulfiram for Alcohol Abstinence. Disulfiram (Antabuse®) reduces the ability of the body to break down alcohol causing a fast accumulation of acetaldehyde. This in turn creates a rapid and highly unpleasant reaction to the ingestion of any alcohol including nausea, flushing, and palpitations. It is best used in patients who are abstinent and compliant, and when facing high-risk situations.

Evidence-Based Approaches—Changing the Individual

As mentioned at the beginning of this chapter, there are a host of agencies and organizations that provide lists of effective or evidence-based programs and approaches. In *What Works in Corrections* (2006) MacKenzie evaluated outcome research of virtually every major treatment method and approach utilized in corrections and criminal justice. The definition of an effective program in MacKenzie's series of meta-analyses is simple. An effective program, or one that "works," is a program that shows a significant and measurable reduction in recidivism. Some of the findings were described in Chapter 13. In the final chapter of the book, MacKenzie concludes that these programs actually work to reduce recidivism:

Academic Education
Vocational Education
Moral Reconation Therapy
Reasoning & Rehabilitation
Cognitive Restructuring
Cognitive Behavioral Treatment of Sex Offenders
Behavioral Treatment of Sex Offenders
Hormonal/Surgical Treatment for Sex Offenders
Multisystemic Therapy for Juveniles
Drug Courts
Community Drug Treatment
Incarceration-Based Drug Treatment

MacKenzie relates that programs "effective in reducing recidivism focus on individual-level change" and adds that cognitive skills and cognitive behavioral programs such as Moral Reconation Therapy lead to changes in the individual that in turn change how the individual relates to others, forming bonds with family, the work world, and institutions. Such changes lead to improved social functioning.

Another large and significant effort to identify evidence-based programs was conducted by the Colorado Division of Criminal Justice in conjunction with the Washington State Institute for Public Policy (Colorado, 2006). Utilizing meta-analysis on published research, most of which was obtained from the National Institute of Corrections, the report attempted to determine an actual percentage of recidivism reduction for various programs and approaches. (The difference between treated offenders and untreated offenders.) The most effective recidivism reduction found in the report was the use of cognitive-behavioral treatment on probationers, which showed a 31.2 percent lower recidivism rate. The next highest recidivism reduction (21.9 percent) was the use of "treatment programs" with intensive supervision (probation). Cognitive-behavioral treatment in prison (14.9 percent) was next followed by vocational education in prisons (12.6 percent), community drug treatment (12.4 percent), adult drug courts (10.7 percent), and cognitive-behavioral programs for general offenders (8.2 percent). A variety of other approaches, many with cognitive-behavioral components, also showed some success at reducing recidivism (ranging from 5 to 7 percent.) MRT outcome research was included in several areas of this report.

Nearly all programs that are effective at reducing recidivism contain some form of cognitive-behavioral treatment component or are completely cognitive-behavioral in nature. Today, it is recognized that virtually all offender groups can benefit from participation in a cognitive-behavioral program.

Chapter 15

Choosing An Evidence-Based Cognitive-Behavioral Program In Criminal Justice

The emphasis of this chapter is on the best choices for an evidence-based program with offenders and substance abusers. The key thing to keep in mind is the overriding issue that offenders have a high level of Antisocial Personality Disorder. Any effective program must target the needs of the offenders and aspects unique to ASPD including criminal thinking, impulsivity, social skills, and other needs. The *Principles of Effective Treatment*, discussed in Chapter 12, should be used as a framework to establish and operate programs. The next chapter of this book contains a series of hints and guidelines for treatment staff in dealing with ASPD clients; however, this chapter concerns establishing an overall cognitive-behavioral program.

There are numerous ways to implement evidence-based programs within any level of the criminal justice system as well as within virtually any treatment setting outside of criminal justice. It has consistently been demonstrated in outcome research that a cognitive component is always found to be a critical part of all treatment programs. Thus, the key point is choosing a specific cognitive component.

What Is Cognitive-Behavioral?

Cognitive-behavioral therapy (CBT) comes from the merger of two different psychological treatment philosophies, cognitive and behavioral theory. Behaviorism focuses on external behaviors and has a long history in treatment dating to the 1920's. Cognitive theory and the emergence of treatments from the concept emphasize the importance of thoughts and thinking (cognition). Cognitive treatment approaches emerged in the 1960's. In the 1980's and 90's, various treatment theorists combined the two approaches into systematic approaches that addressed specific problem areas, such as anxiety, depression, and eventually into criminal behavior areas. In the simplest of terminology, cognitive-behavioral therapy focuses on what a person actually does and how that person thinks and makes decisions. It is a "here-and-now" approach that seldom delves to any great degree into the past, nor does it attempt to make people feel better about themselves, or use the core client-centered counseling techniques.

Cognitive-Behavioral Treatment—A Simple Example. One of the easiest ways to understand the cognitive-behavioral approach is to give a simple example of just one of its ways to deal with depression. People who are depressed perceive (or know) that they are depressed and then they will act depressed. This "depressed-like" behavior in turn confirms that they really are depressed, leading to more behaviors showing depression. And on and on it goes. The thoughts about being depressed reinforce and produce the behaviors of depression, which confirm and reinforce the thoughts about being depressed, leading to even more behaviors associated with depression. A depressed person might say, "I am depressed and tired, so I'll just lie here and sleep." So the individual reduces activity, engages in other activities associated with what the person believes is depression, and then feels more depressed and often even more tired. Depression is a vicious cycle recognized by treatment providers and many depressed individuals alike. This type of depression can be directly addressed by asking, "What would you normally do if you were not depressed?" The person might say "exercise, take a walk, go out with friends." The homework assignment that might be assigned by a cognitive-behavioral therapist would be to have the depressed person engage in one of the behaviors that would normally be done if the person wasn't depressed. In short, the individual would be told to "act as if" he or she wasn't depressed, but in a systematic step-by-step fashion. Such behavioral assignments typically start small and are related to real-life behaviors. Depressed individuals might be assigned to wash their clothes or car, go out to eat with a friend, mow the lawn, or exercise. At the same time they are asked to list specific thoughts and ideas they have about their depression. Gradually as the person acts more and more as if he or she is not depressed, and the person comes to understand the self-defeating thoughts and beliefs that pop into his or her mind, the depression lifts. A substantial amount of research shows that this cognitive-behavioral approach can actually alter brain chemistry and create lasting changes in brain cell connections.

As cognitive-behavioral programs pertain to offenders, only a few of these programs use this approach by systematically addressing the beliefs, attitudes, and behaviors associated with criminality. Moral Reconation Therapy, or MRT, does just this by starting with one of the fundamental underpinnings of ASPD—lying. MRT starts by having offenders "act as if" they are not liars by having them be honest about the only thing that the program can be certain is true. That is, they must admit that they have lied. Then they are encouraged and reinforced for behaviors that show honesty. From that point, the program requires a series of treatment activities that address such issues as trust, basic acceptance of rules, looking at damaged relationships, and so on. It is a progressive, step-by-step approach to dismantle criminal thinking and establish behaviors not typically found with ASPDs. A good cognitive-behavioral program will be shown to be effective because the participants will gradually act less and less like ASPDs and more and more "normal." In sum, the behaviors associated with ASPD and criminality will be addressed while more appropriate behaviors are required, and that is done in conjunction with dismantling criminal thinking.

Programmatic Options

We recommend using the NREPP list to identify and evaluate potential programs; however, in general criminal justice there are various other factors that are considered. Programs are not always chosen because they work, are evidence-based, or are effective. Sometimes programs are chosen because they are inexpensive or made attractive by advertising and slick marketing. Politics, personalities, likes and dislikes, prejudice, and cost are all factors that many agencies consider in choosing what programs, if any, they will offer. Virtually all publications on evidence-based programs recommend that program decision-makers be informed consumers and make choices based on reliable and valid information. In addition, ongoing evaluation of programs must occur and changes should be made where necessary. Only one NREPP cognitive-behavioral program is listed for both adults and juveniles for all levels of criminal justice treatment—Moral Reconation Therapy® or MRT (the present authors' program)—but there are other NREPP programs for more specific behavioral targets (e.g., juveniles, mental health, dual-diagnosis, etc.). In a 2007 National Institute of Corrections Publication titled *Cognitive-Behavioral Treatment: A Review and Discussion for Corrections Professionals* (Milkman & Wanberg, 2007) six programs were discussed. One was for anger control while another focused on relapse prevention. These will not be discussed. Four general cognitive-behavioral programs were listed in the NIC publication as current "evidence-based" options for correctional populations: 1) Wanberg and Milkman's own Strategies for Self-Improvement and Change (SSC); 2) Reasoning & Rehabilitation; 3) Thinking for a Change; and 4) Moral Reconation Therapy.

Strategies for Self-Improvement and Change (SSC). SSC was developed by Wanberg and Milkman as described as "a standardized, structured, and well-defined approach to the treatment of clients who manifest substance abuse and criminal justice problems. It is a long-term (9 months to 1 year), intensive, cognitive-behavioral-oriented treatment program for adult substance-abusing offenders. The recommended client age is 18 years or older."

The program's effectiveness has been reported in a single study (Wanberg & Milkman, 2001) using self-reported data from clients and client ratings from providers. Treatment staff rated clients as more abstinent during treatment and having "fair to very good prognosis." As of February 2010, SSC has not been granted NREPP status.

Reasoning & Rehabilitation (R & R). R & R was developed by Robert Ross and Elizabeth Fabiano in 1985 at the University of Ottawa (Canada) with the text, *Time to Think: A Cognitive Model of Delinquency Prevention and Offender Rehabilitation* (1985) providing the foundation of the program. The initial implementation was with probationers in Ontario, Canada. "This program focuses on enhancing self-control, interpersonal problem solving, social perspectives, and prosocial attitudes and consists of 35 sessions, running from 8 to 12 weeks, with 6 to 8 participants." In 1996 a short version of the program was developed and termed R & R2. The 2007 NIC *Cognitive Behavioral Treatment* publication cites seven outcome studies on R & R relating "that results were mixed, with the scientifically higher quality studies finding that R & R resulted in lower rates of reoffense... [and] one was not statistically significant with R & R participants' recidivism rate at 26 percent compared to a rate of 29 percent for non-R & R participants." R & R was extensively employed in England with several outcome studies performed. Falshaw, *et al.* (2004) compiled a large 2-year recidivism study on 649 R & R-treated offenders and a control group of 1,947. They found "no significant differences in two-year reconviction rates between the treatment and matched comparison groups in any of the risk categories." The R & R-treated group showed a 39.4 percent reconviction rate as compared to a *lower* rate of 39.2 percent in the controls. Wilkinson (2005) found the opposite of what was expected: "His findings showed that 76 percent of the R & R group were reconvicted within 2 years as compared to 56 percent of untreated offenders" and wrote "It would seem that R & R did not reduce offending." Oddly, the study reported, "Offenders whose attitudes changed prosocially were more likely to be reconvicted than were offenders whose attitudes did not change positively," adding "Evidence the programme achieves significant reductions in offending is questionable." There are also findings that R & R does not fare well with minority groups. As of February 2010, R & R has not been granted NREPP status.

Thinking for a Change (T4C). T4C was developed in 1997 as an initiative by the National Institute of Corrections. Because of its association with the NIC, the program was quickly implemented widely and is now found in over 40 states in hundreds of locations. The program is designed to increase offenders' awareness of self and others through social skills and problem-solving activities. It is performed in small groups (8 to 12 individuals) and consists of 22 one to two hour lessons. There are 10 additional sessions that are typically recommended. Despite its wide implementation since 1997 and its active promotion as being "evidence-based," only two outcome studies have been publishedon T4C to date. The first was a dissertation (Golden, 2002) that studied 42 adult offenders on probation. The study divided the

T4C participants into completers and dropouts and also had a small control group. Self-reports, treatment staff ratings, and recidivism were measured at 3 months and one year. Results showed that the 3-month recidivism rate (new criminal offenses) for T4C participants was 15.5% compared to 20% for controls, but it was not statistically significant. There were no differences between any of the groups in technical violations. Testing measures of procriminal attitudes showed no differences among the groups after treatment. A second and larger study on T4C was conducted on 233 probationers (Lowenkamp and Latessa, 2006). Again, the study evaluated program completers and compared them to dropouts as well as to a control group. No definitive time period for the recidivism analysis was used (such as one year); however, the participants and controls were assessed for rearrests after an average of 26 months, with a range of 6 to 64 months. Results showed all T4C participants had a recidivism rate of 23 percent compared to a 35 percent rate for controls. As of February 2010, T4C has not been granted NREPP status.

Moral Reconation Therapy (MRT). MRT was gradually developed by the authors of this text in a series of brief group programs at several prisons with ongoing research evaluating various outcomes. The program was fully implemented within a prison-based drug treatment TC in 1985 (Little & Robinson, 1988). The workbook *How To Escape Your Prison* (Little & Robinson, 1986) contains a series of exercise and homework assignments which participants complete and share in groups. The program generally consists of 20 to 32 group sessions conducted once or twice a week and lasting 1 to 2 hours per session. The number of participants in groups varies from 8 to more than 40. Versions of the book have been developed for adults and juveniles. MRT is aimed at general offenders, substance abusers, and DUI/DWI offenders. Other versions of MRT have been developed for anger management, domestic violence, sex offenders, parenting, and relapse prevention. The program has been widely implemented in every level of criminal justice including prisons, jails, probation and parole, community corrections, juvenile justice, and drug courts. It is in use in nearly every state and several different countries. Over 120 outcome studies have been published on MRT making it the most researched of all available cognitive-behavioral systems utilized with offenders. All but one of the studies reported lower recidivism and a host of other beneficial results. A 10-year recidivism study evaluating 115 multiple DWI offenders treated with MRT and 65 matched controls showed that the treated group's 10-year reincarceration rate was 44.4 percent as compared to 61.5 percent in the controls. The treated DWI offenders' reincarceration rate was significantly lower (Little, *et al.,* 1999). A similar 10-year recidivism study was conducted on 1,052 MRT-treated felony offenders who were compared to 329 nontreated controls (Little, *et al.,* 1999a). Results showed that the MRT-treated group was significantly lower in recidivism rates for each of the 10 years. At the 10th year after release, the MRT-treated group showed a 45 percent reincarceration rate as compared to 64 percent for nontreated controls. A 20-year recidivism study on the same 1,052 MRT-treated offenders and 329 controls was published in 2010 (Little, *et al.,* 2010). Results showed that 94% of the nontreated controls had been rearrested over the 20 years of release as compared to 81% of the MRT-treated offenders. Over 82% of the controls had been reincarcerated during the same time period as compared to 61% of the MRT-treated offenders. Both results were statistically significant. To our knowledge, MRT is the only offender cognitive-behavioral treatment system that has 10 and 20-year outcome data. As of February 2010, MRT is the only cognitive-behavioral program for general offender groups that has been granted NREPP status. MRT has been granted NREPP status in substance abuse treatment, corrections, and with co-occurring disorders.

Cognitive-Behavioral
Program Implementation Strategies

Cognitive-behavioral programs can be implemented within every level of criminal justice. These include specialized programs as well as with general offender populations. Note that the initial step is to choose a program that fits the site and type of offender and that training in all of the techniques is necessary. The following section outlines how programs are performed at various sites.

Probation & Parole

Parole and probation remain the setting where the vast majority of offenders "serve" their sentence. Many parole and probation officers work only in supervisory roles, essentially as a specialized police force with individual caseloads. It is common practice for probationers and parolees in need of substance abuse treatment to be referred to outside agencies for the service. Other needs, be it educational, vocational, or social are also typically addressed through referral. Such a system can be effective; however, the implementation of a cognitive-behavioral program within the agency can be beneficial. Many probation and parole agencies provide cognitive-behavioral programs to their clients in weekly groups operated by the officers. Offenders are either identified as high-risk or simply automatically assigned to such programs upon entry. A 2005 meta-analysis of MRT employed in parole and probation sites evaluated 9 outcome reports that included 2,460 MRT-treated offenders and 7,679 nontreated controls (Little, 2005). The treated groups' recidivism was over 22 percent lower than the nontreated controls. The employment of a cognitive-behavioral program in parole and probation gives the officers a unique supervision technique that leads to better supervision and lower recidivism.

Drug Courts & Other Specialized Courts

Specialized drug courts are a relatively new phenomenon. In 1989 there was only one American drug court, and in 1999 there were 472; yet in 2007 an astonishing 2,147 drug courts were operating (Huddleston, *et al.*, 2008). Drug courts are designed to provide specialized coerced treatment as well as intense supervision, and they are an alternative to incarceration. There are specialized courts for adults and juveniles. Cognitive programming for drug court participants is generally conducted by private contractors or drug court staff in weekly groups. A National Drug Court Institute publication (Hardin & Kushner, 2008) focused on employing evidence-based practices in drug courts. While many drug courts contract direct substance abuse services for their clients through outside providers, many require the use of cognitive programs, especially cognitive-behavioral relapse prevention. The effectiveness of drug courts is well established (Hora & Stalcup, 2008).

While most drug courts evaluate the difference between their program completers with dropouts, there is substantial evidence that drug court participation lowers the recidivism of program participants. A 2006 study (Little, 2006) reviewed the outcomes of 18 adult drug courts and 11 juvenile drug courts, all of which used MRT as their cognitive component. All showed lower recidivism and other beneficial effects. Because of the success of drug courts, several variations of these have emerged including family courts, domestic abuse courts, DUI courts, and Native American Tribal courts, all of which typically employ a general cognitive-behavioral approach in addition to their other methods. More recently (Kirchner & Goodman, 2007; Kirchner & Kirchner, 2008; McCabe, 2009; McCracken, Hearn, & Stuckey, 2003) have reported on the success of MRT in reducing recidivism in drug and wellness courts in Thurston County, WA; Putnam County, FL; Anchorage, AK; and in Albuquerque, NM.

Prisons & Jails (General Offender Populations)

Cognitive-behavioral programs are typically offered to general offender populations by institutional staff who have been trained in the specific method chosen. The staff varies from counselors to correctional officers as well as educational staff. A few institutions utilize outside contractors to conduct the scheduled groups. Such programs are offered because the leaders of the specific institution want to reduce recidivism, reduce inmate infractions, and provide rehabilitation activities. The groups are usually weekly or twice weekly and offenders simply attend their scheduled groups. Numerous large studies have been conducted on the utilization of MRT with general offender groups. MacKenzie (2006) evaluated four such studies on MRT and concluded, "the research provides strong evidence that MRT programs are effective in reducing the recidivism of offenders."

Community Corrections

Community corrections has become a wide-ranging term that includes private probation, alternate housing of offenders, private treatment services, and numerous specialized services. The industry is a fast-expanding area in corrections because it can be cost-effective and occasionally funded by the offenders themselves. In recent years it has become more common that community corrections agencies provide specific services stipulated by courts or other referral agencies. Many community corrections agencies do provide cognitive-behavioral programming in specialized group formats. These agencies provide cognitive-behavioral programs focusing on substance abuse, domestic violence, anger management, shoplifting, underage drinking, parenting, and a host of general offender programs such as MRT.

Educational & Vocational Programs

Educational and vocational programming aimed at offenders has a purpose that transcends reducding recidivism. While recidivism reduction should always be a goal of corrections, there is perhaps a moral imperative to provide education and vocational programs for this population. This is especially true with offenders with ASPD, as low education and poor job skills are characteristics of that population. In recent years many corrections-based educational and vocational staff have recognized that the attitudes, beliefs, and behaviors typical of offender populations are key areas that have to be addressed in order for a long-term effect to be realized. Many teachers and instructors in these

programs now conduct cognitive-behavioral groups with their students. While there is not a substantial amount of research on this approach, several large implementations have conducted some outcome evaluations. Delaware's Life Skills Program employed MRT within their program (Miller & Hobler, 1996; Miller, 1997) and found that MRT participants had a 76 percent success rate on work release as opposed to 52 percent for non-MRT work release participants. A unique use of MRT began at Tidewater Community College in 1997 (Broughton, 2004). In a "Welfare to Work" program designed to transition welfare recipients into jobs, over 600 individuals graduated from the program after completing MRT. The program's dropout rate was 21 percent compared to a 28 percent national dropout rate in similar programs. After completing the program, 95 percent were placed in jobs.

Therapeutic Communities (TC)

Early research on treating incarcerated substance abusers showed that purely behavioral management techniques and group therapies utilized within the therapeutic community (TC) reduced subsequent substance use and recidivism to a small, but significant, degree (Martinson, 1971; Sweet, *et al.*, 1979). TCs are found in prisons and in some community corrections facilities. They are closed residential communities where the participants live, work, and engage in continuing treatment activities with little or no interaction with outsiders. In essence, it is a method that immerses the participant in ongoing treatment and has some parallels to residential hospital-based treatment programs. TCs have rigid rules and a rigid structure, a peer hierarchy, and they use rein-

forcement and punishment techniques along with various group activities. TCs have operated for over 40 years and research on over 65,000 treated participants has shown that TCs are "associated with positive outcomes" (NIDA, 2002).

The authors of this text first became involved in a prison-based drug treatment TC in 1976 at the Shelby County Correction Center in Memphis, Tennessee, which then used a strictly behavioral approach termed *Reconation Therapy* (Wood & Sweet, 1974). The term *reconation* comes from *conation*, which was used to describe the decision-making process prior to the popularization of the term *ego* around 1930. A comprehensive report on the program (Sweet, *et al.,* 1977) showed that program completers had a much lower recidivism rate than dropouts and controls; however the dropout rate was high, a problem noted in virtually all TCs. Subsequent analyses showed that blacks had a significantly higher dropout rate than whites (Little, 1981) and that those most likely to dropout quickly were younger, had low education levels, were racial minorities, and tended to prefer cocaine and its derivatives (Little & Robinson, 1987; Robinson & Little, 1982). That same research employed MMPI testing and showed that nearly all of the program's participants were antisocial and that the stronger the antisocial traits were, the more likely the individual was to drop out. Catego-

rizing the fundamental traits of ASPD found in the offenders, the authors constructed a set of exercises that progressively addressed the behaviors and attitudes underlying each antisocial trait in a unique manner. This was done in order to directly present the attitudes and beliefs that antisocial behaviors are based upon and then paradoxically to have the offender dismantle the reasoning and change their behavior. The initial phase of testing this developing cognitive-behavioral approach was piloted at the Federal Correctional Institution in Memphis in 1979-83. In the mid-1980's, the present authors installed and researched the newly-developed cognitive program, which by then had added the concept of moral reasoning as presented by psychologist Lawrence Kohlberg. The overall program was formed into a workbook with progressive exercises and was implemented in such a way that each participant could work at his own pace and new clients could enter the program at any time. This aspect of the system is called open-ended groups as opposed to an educational class setting where all participants work on the same lessons at the same time—which is a major limitation of many treatment approaches. Because the program was based on Kohlberg's moral reasoning levels and it was first employed in the TC

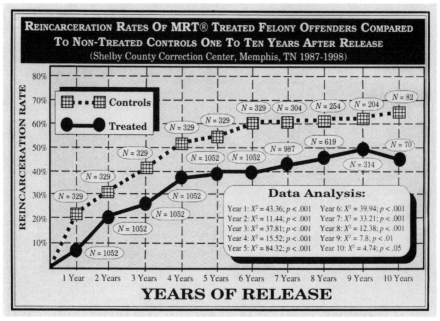

Ten-Year Recidivism Outcome of MRT-Treated Offenders
Source: Little, *et al.*, 1999.

utilizing Reconation Therapy, the now trademarked cognitive-behavioral approach was termed *Moral Reconation Therapy* or MRT.

The first comprehensive report on the approach was published three years after full implementation (Little & Robinson, 1988). Results showed that minority (African American) participation in the program increased by 33 percent; minority completion rates increased by 86 percent; and completion by whites increased by 62 percent. A TC for multiple-DWI offenders was then established in the same institution using MRT, and a specialized aftercare program was established for both the DWI and drug TC participants also utilizing MRT. This was, to our knowledge, the first use of a "continuum of care" in corrections. A series of outcome studies detailed the results from both the DWI TC and drug treatment TC. The reports detailed changes in a host of personality test variables as well as rearrest status, and reincarceration status for a full twenty years after participants were released from the institution. In addition, all program participants, whether they were completers or dropouts, were included in the analyses and various quasi-experimental control groups were formed. To our knowledge, the use

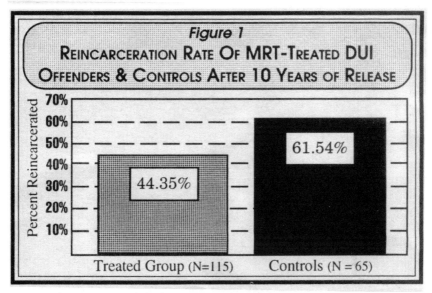

Ten-Year Recidivism Outcome of MRT-Treated DUI Offenders
Source: Little, *et al.*, 1999.

of MRT in a parole and probation aftercare program (where it was started in a prison) was the first use of a strictly cognitive-behavioral program with such offenders. In brief, MRT participants showed a rearrest and reincarceration rate of less than half that of appropriate control groups for the initial three years after release. From that time until 10 years after their release, the MRT participants consistently showed a recidivism rate (including both rearrests and reincarceration) 25 to 33 percent lower than the controls. To date, over 120 outcome studies have been published on MRT making it the most researched offender-intended cognitive-behavioral program. A 2006 report detailed over 20 outcome studies using MRT in TCs for females, juveniles, and adults, all showing significant and desired reductions in recidivism and other variables. MacKenzie (2006) cites TCs as a correctional approach that actually works to significantly reduce recidivism.

The main drawbacks to TCs include their high staff-to-participant ratio (cost), the need for specialized and highly competent staff, and their intensity, meaning that TCs often have high dropout rates. However, TCs remain the favored and most appropriate approach for treating substance-abusing offenders who are incarcerated.

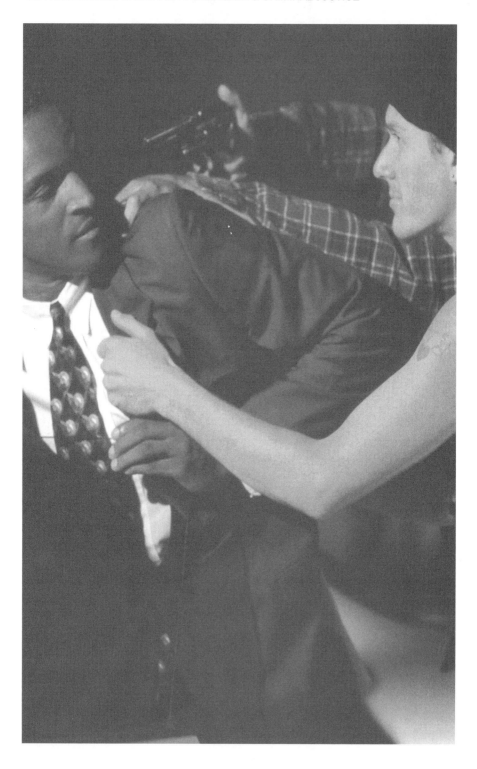

Chapter 16

Hints In Dealing
With ASPD Offenders

It should be clear that clients with ASPD must be treated in different ways than non-ASPD substance abusers for treatment to have a beneficial and lasting impact. Because verbal interactions remain the most frequent type of communication between staff and offenders, we have compiled a list of hints for treatment staff and those dealing with offenders and substance abusers.

1. Dealing With Victim's Issues And Statements

It is certainly true that some people were victimized by their parents, schools, their military service, and by society because of prejudice and other factors. Ask yourself, *"What can I do to change these things in this client's past?"* If the answer is *nothing* except make them accept it and maybe feel better about it, then it's not an issue that can be treated. **Keep *them* focused on changing things *now* in an active, present-time sense.** Also remember that many clients use victim's statements to manipulate the treatment providers and gain sympathy or shirk responsibility. For example, one way of manipulating staff and the system with victim's statements is by claiming childhood sexual abuse.

A clever study (Hindman, 1988) was conducted on offenders to assess the incidence of childhood sexual abuse. Prior to her introduction of a lie detector in the clinic, Hindman found that 67% of sex offenders reported that they were sexually victimized during their childhood. In addition, only 29% reported that they began offending during their adolescence. After the lie detector was moved into the clinic, only 21% reported they had been victimized during their childhood and 71% reported that they had begun abusing others during their childhood or adolescence. Another study (Resnick, Foy, Donahoe, & Miller, 1989) assessed the incidence of ASPD in Vietnam vets who entered treatment for Post-Traumatic Stress Disorder caused by combat exposure. While the study verified that exposure to certain types and periods of combat can produce PTSD, it was also found that pre-existing ASPD in the vets was significantly correlated to post-combat antisocial behaviors.

The implications of such research on treatment are that many ASPD clients use victim's statements as a means of subtle manipulation of treatment staff and as a means of shirking responsibility for their behavior. Thus, when programs explore the client's past with the client, the client believes that treatment staff *wants* to find something to blame their current antisocial behavior upon. Such methods are counterproductive with ASPDs and are to be avoided. The issue to keep in mind is to ask yourself if there is something you can do to change this event in the client's past? If not, it may not be something you should address or explore. In addition, with some exceptions, if you find yourself asking questions that elicit victim's statements, and if you are not prepared to deal with the issue that arises, it is not necessarily a good thing to bring it up.

2. Remember That Abusers Referred From Criminal Justice Are Not That Different From Abusers Who Were Not Referred From Criminal Justice

Data shows that many substance abusers and alcoholics are antisocial. While some chemical dependency counselors do not like to view their clients as "criminals" or as antisocial, the two groups are more similar than they might appear. Also remember that all those who have ASPD are not necessarily criminals — the two descriptive terms (ASPD & Criminal Personality) are not necessarily synonymous. A study referred to earlier (Farabee, Nelson, & Spence, 1993) compared substance abusers who entered an outpatient treatment program from criminal justice referrals to those who entered from other sources. The study compared the two groups on 11 psychosocial variables. In seven of the variables, *the two groups were virtually identical.* The criminal justice clients, however, showed *better* decision-making than the voluntary admissions. Other variables revealed that the criminal justice clients see their substance abuse as *less of a problem;* they have *less desire for help* with their substance abuse behaviors; and they are less ready for treatment. This should not be surprising since ASPDs do not view themselves as having a problem—the problem is always with the system, society, or the laws.

3. Substance Abusers With ASPD Think Differently

It should be apparent at this point that ASPD clients do not see themselves as having much of a problem with drugs. Thus, it is not surprising that they don't really want help and are "less ready for treatment." In his now-classic book based on Samuel Yochelson's work with criminals, *Inside The Criminal Mind (1984),* Stanton Samenow says it bluntly: *"The essence of this approach is that criminals choose to commit crimes. Crime resides within the person and is 'caused' by the way he thinks, not by his environment. Criminals think differently from responsible people... Focusing on forces outside the criminal is futile... From regarding criminals as victims we saw that instead they were victimizers who had freely chosen their way of life... Criminals know right from wrong. In fact, some know the law better than their lawyers.* **But they believe that whatever they want to do at any given time is right for them"** (pp. xiv-xv; 10-11).

In support of this statement, research has confirmed that offenders and substance abusers show lower levels of moral reasoning than others. Research on MRT has shown that its effectiveness is derived in part by raising moral reasoning. Pugh (1993) echoes this finding in his research when he stresses that offenders have deviant values and need approaches that "promote moral development." Spiecker (1988) identified a lack of moral emotions as a key element in ASPD clients. Others have also found that moral reasoning deficits are present in substance-abusing juvenile offenders (Morgan, Eagle, Esser, & Roth, 1993) and that relatively high moral reasoning serves as a deterrence to criminal behavior (Veneziano & Veneziano, 1992).

A simple common example of how ASPD thinking works can be seen with many of those who are arrested for DWI and then are forced into some form of treatment. Many of the convicted drunk drivers choose to repeatedly argue with treatment personnel that the DWI laws are unfair. "It's not fair," they state repeatedly rather than choosing to look at how their behavior might have threatened others. Interestingly, the moral reasoning of convicted drunk drivers is often less than that of those convicted of felony offences (Little & Robinson, 1989).

A key issue in this discussion is the inappropriate application of "normal reasoning" to offenders. Normal people (those without a diagnosis) will usually respond well to educational opportunities and vocational opportunities. Seeing that offender populations lack education and vocational skills, the logical thinking is that education and vocational training is what is needed. But there are reasons why offenders, especially those with ASPD, have low education and poor vocational skills. The reason is in how they view education and work—and their thinking and beliefs are not what we would call "normal."

In sum, the ASPD does whatever he or she wants to do, including substance abuse, because that *is simply what he or she chooses to do.* There is little concern for others only for themselves and their immediate gratification. Successful approaches to treat ASPDs have focused on changing how offenders think and make their decisions. Unsuccessful approaches to ASPD focus on exploring their feelings and their past.

4. Make Their Behavior The Focus

Offenders can often engage in discussions about how the system is run by white-collar criminals and that others lie, cheat, and steal. In fact, they will attempt to get staff to admit that they once stole something, lied, or cheated. DWI offenders will give examples of how "everybody" drinks and drives and how they "just got caught." They will go out of their way to get staff to admit that they too have had times when they drank and then drove. These are attempts to level the playing field and make the argument that they are no different than others. Keep in mind that lying is common, but consistent lying to take advantage of others is a characteristic of ASPD. The focus needs to remain on the offenders' behavior and beliefs. A way to deal with such issues is to say something like, "Sure, other people have gotten away with stealing, and when they get here they will be treated the same way. But you are here, and they are not." When it comes to the drinking and driving argument, it's probably true that many people, including corrections staff, have drank and then driven. The appropriate reply is: "If

I had been caught, I'd be dealt with the same way, and if and when anyone else comes in, they'll be treated the same way. But right now you are here. We need to focus on you."

5. Understand That A Minority Of ASPD Clients Are Dangerous

It is true that past behavior is often the best predictor of possible future behavior. Thus, clients who have shown a history of violence tend to have a greater likelihood of future violence. Many substance abuse counselors hesitate treating criminal substance abusers due to their fear of violence. Dealing with potentially violent ASPDs requires consistency in enforcing rules and a certainty of what is expected of them, in conjunction with a certainty of the consequences of their actions. In terms of assessing a client's propensity toward dangerous violence, Tobey & Bruhn (1992) have found that the prediction of violent clients can be reliably indicated by the number of the early life memories of emotional and physical violence that clients have when asked to recall the four earliest events in their lives. In general, violent clients recalled 3 or 4 severe, violent events which typically happened at home and to them during their childhood. Criminals found to be nonviolent typically recalled two or fewer such events that were less severe. Some ASPD clients that abuse drugs and alcohol are violent — especially in their battering of those they supposedly love. The last chapter will address this specialized area of treatment.

6. Remember That ASPD Can Coexist With Other Diagnoses

DSM-IV-TR diagnosis is a mystery to many substance abuse counselors. It is probably a good idea to review the many other possible diagnoses that substance-abusing clients can have. For example, studies have found that 30% to 40% of those diagnosed with Major Depression also have a Personality Disorder (see Shea, Widiger, & Klein, 1992 for a review of depression and PD). Also recall that studies have shown that from one-third to two-thirds of those entering chemical abuse treatment probably have a Personality Disorder. Thus, treating only the depression will not typically do anything beneficial to ASPD symptoms. In fact, relieving depression in an ASPD client could potentially increase their antisocial behavior. This is not to say that treating depression in ASPD isn't warranted; it simply means that some other interventions must also be used.

7. Be Consistent And Firm In Enforcing Rules

ASPDs seek out and notice inconsistencies in others' behavior as justification for their own actions. It is inconceivable that treatment staff could be observed lying, drunk or under the influence, or showing favoritism toward certain clients and then not expect the client to do the same. When ASPDs observe staff making excuses, claiming to be victims, and focusing on their own feelings, the ASPDs' worldview is reinforced. Learn to follow and enforce the rules consistently and firmly. When clients say, "Rules are made to be broken," reply "Rules are made to be followed."

8. Don't Engage In Philosophical Arguments About Fairness

ASPDs are experts at pointing out how unfair the world is to them and others. If they can get you to agree with them, they can and will justify their actions based on the opinion (which you have agreed with) that the world is unfair and must be resisted. Keep the focus on *their* situation and what is expected of them, and on the consequences of their behavior. Arguing the fairness of DWI laws or drug laws with an ASPD is pointless. The simple fact is that they want to get high or drunk and do not want anyone to bother them. Fairness is not the real issue with them — their personal pleasure is. However, the unfairness argument is part of their defense mechanisms and justification for their behavior. The simple solution to this is to refuse to engage in such discussions and focus on their behavior in the program and the consequences of their behavior.

9. Refrain From The Use Of Treatment Jargon

ASPDs will quickly learn to manipulate with the use of treatment terminology and jargon. Speak in simple, common terms.

Unfortunately, clients begin to use jargon so they do not really have to discuss what is happening at a deeper level. Terminology and jargon are for professionals to more efficiently communicate with each other. If a client uses jargon, ask the person to define exactly what the term means. For example, a client might say that they agree that they "minimize and justify" their actions. What an ASPD means by that statement is not what a treatment professional means. They mean that the issue is trivial and they are not really going to change because they have justified their actions.

10. Understand That Punishment Does Not Affect ASPDs As It Does Others

Findings that ASPDs do not profit from experience are consistent and stem in part from their failure to learn from punishment. First, ASPDs do not experience fear and anxiety as non-ASPDs do. A vast number of psychophysiological studies show that there are actual physical and biological differences in how they experience fear, threats, and stress. The things "normal" people fear do not have the same effect on ASPDs. In addition, many ASPDs do not appear to connect the behaviors they perform to the punishments they receive. Instead, they blame getting caught and blame "unfair" rules. A relatively recent theory (Sherman, 1993) explains how punishment can even increase crime as many studies have shown. *The Defiance Theory* postulates that the presence of four conditions leads to defiance of laws, society, and authority. These are: 1) An offender defines a punishment as unfair (whether because the laws are unjust, others get away with it, or it is established by an unjust society); 2) The offender is alienated or unattached to the community or authority issuing the punishment; 3) The offender sees the punishment as stigmatizing and rejecting them personally; and 4) The offender refuses to acknowledge shame from the punishment. Thus, *stigmatizing punishments from a distant authority (with which the offender has no bonds) are deemed unfair and inconsistent and cause offenders no shame.* In fact, punishments perceived as "unfair" may actually increase the offender's rage, make him or her see society as even more unfair and view sanctions as irrelevant and unfair, and raise defiance in future behavior. So, sanctions on treated ASPDs must be handled in an evenhanded, consistent fashion. In addition, the necessity and importance of shame associated with wrongful conduct must be used as a treatment tool with ASPDs.

11. Use Methods Appropriate To The ASPD Client

Substance abuse counselors who are frustrated with clients from the criminal justice system are most likely using inappropriate treatment strategies. Searching the past, psychotherapy, treating abuses suffered during their childhood, discussing how unfair the world is, blaming others and looking for deep-seated reasons for client behavior, and client-centered approaches are all inappropriate or ineffective with

ASPDs. The use of AA or other such self-help groups is inexpensive (actually free) but yields no measurable reduction in recidivism. However, such self-help programs should be offered and encouraged as they do create an outside support system. Programs suffering high dropout rates with ASPDs are also using ineffective and inappropriate methods.

Taking Aim at Antisocial Thinking & Behaviors: Specific Hints

Various theorists have identified the most frequent thinking and behavioral errors made by antisocials. Below we have listed some of the most frequently discussed issues in ASPD thinking and behavior along with specific suggestions to cope with them:

1. ASPDs tend to have a criminal or negative self-identity. That is, they think of themselves as a "druggie," a "gangster," a "rebel," or "tough." Effective programming must reverse this image by having clients perform more positive activities and expose them to role models whom they respect and who have a more positive identity. It is essential that group and individual programming strive to develop and maintain positive identity.

2. ASPDs tend to think that others cannot be trusted and are dishonest just as they are. Programs must show the ASPD clients, through the staff's behavior and the way they run the program, that program staff can be trusted and are honest. Honesty, trust, and consistency must be held in high respect by the program itself. Staff who make excuses for being late, violating rules, and having bad attitudes only reinforce the worst characteristics of ASPDs.

3. ASPDs are impulsive and lack internal controls. Effective programs must require that clients maintain positive behavior indefinitely and earn privileges through sustained positive behavior. Time-based rewards are necessary for this to occur, and frustration tolerance builds as clients have to "wait" for rewards. A behavioristic approach is very useful to achieve this.

4. Self-awareness is poor in ASPDs. Programs must show the clients how it is their behavior that gets them into trouble, *not* that they get caught. ASPDs must learn to take responsibility for their actions and those that they have hurt. They must also come to realize what they have to do to reverse their choices in life.

5. ASPDs are often apathetic and indifferent. Programs must force (through rules) clients to behave "as if" they cared about others. ASPDs do not believe that they have to change, so programs must reward them for changing. You must show *them the wisdom of change and having some conformity to rules.* Over time and experience they will receive some rewards for good behavior and it will become more ingrained.

6. ASPDs tend to have negative peers and associates. Clients must come to understand and accept that the people they most trust *can not be trusted* and those they trust the least *can* be trusted. Their peers and associates tend to lead them into trouble, and the price of "loyalty" to their friends is pain and suffering. Programs must show clients the path to developing more positive peers and relationships. Obviously program staff must show that they are trustworthy.

7. ASPDs do not like to deal with real life. ASPDs want what they want instantly. They do not like to work for it and would just as soon take it from someone else. Program rules must stress the importance of real-life activities and show clients the wisdom of following rules and being consistent in handling the constant problems that emerge in day-to-day life.

8. Be on the ASPDs' side. ASPDs are accustomed to being against society, programs, and rules and having others oppose them. Tell them you are on their side and show them you want them to be successful. In your occupation you should wish for their success.

9. Reward their successes in the program and reward them for following the rules. Establish a group procedure for making a big deal out of client accomplishments — whether it is the giving of a small, tangible reward or a round of applause.

10. Maintain a positive peer pressure. Hold group participants accountable when they don't discuss issues (call it "nonconcern") or act disinterested. Verbally praise clients for making statements wherein they show concern for others (not remorse). Do not allow negative peer comments to go unchallenged.

11. Have clients assess themselves as if they are assessing another client. Have them list their strengths and weaknesses and make suggestions for improvements. ASPDs like picking others apart and are often quite good at it. If you can get them to pick apart someone "who acts and thinks just like they do," they will eventually begin to change as they come to see themselves in others.

12. Be blunt and confrontive in a manner that lets them know you care (that you are on their side). Many counselors find being blunt and confrontive difficult but need to understand that clients will not break and that they usually appreciate the bluntness. "Blunt" does not mean "cruel," it simply means being honest.

Chapter 17

Special Correctional Populations: Batterers, Female Offenders, & Mental Health

In recent years the issue of domestic violence and battering has become more important and noticeable. About 5% of men batter women and a much smaller number of women batter their significant other. Most batterers programs are based upon the assumption that battering is the man's attempt to gain power and control over a woman. This assumption has been validated by research from as early as 1980 (National Institute of Justice, 1995). Alcohol use is typically present in battering cases, but researchers and treatment providers are quick to emphasize that battering is not caused by alcohol. Data indicates that 76% of batterers self-report alcohol problems and 65% show the alcohol dependence diagnosis. Over 70% show a drug dependence diagnosis. The use of drugs and alcohol by batterers parallels that of ASPDs. Research on batterers' personality and behavioral characteristics has uncovered three distinct subtypes or clusters of perpetrators of domestic violence.

One subtype, sometimes called the *Typical Batterer* or the *Second Cluster,* tends to batter only when drinking and nearly always shows remorse. Approximately 25% of batterers fall into this cluster. It is likely that this subgroup does not represent ASPD diagnoses.

The so-called *Antisocial Batterer,* also referred to as the *First Cluster,* tends to be angry, jealous, shows little remorse, uses severe forms of violence, and abuses drugs and or alcohol. This subgroup usually has a criminal record in addition to the battering and is, in all probability, characterized by ASPD.

The Third Cluster, sometimes called the *Sociopathic Batterer,* is the most violent of the three groups and perpetrates violent acts frequently and to various persons. This subgroup tends to report abuse as a child, abuses drugs and alcohol, shows little jealousy and anger, shows no remorse, and has a long and varied criminal record. Persons in this grouping also have a high probability of being ASPD.

Research on batterers has also focused on diagnosing personality disorders. In a paper presented at the American Society of Criminology in 1986, Hamberger and Hastings reported that 80% of wife assaulters have diagnosable personality disorders. Hart, Dutton, & Newlove (1993) found that 90% of batterers were diagnosable with personality disorders based on personality tests. Dutton and Starzomski (1994) assessed differences in diagnoses in groups of batterers referred to treatment from criminal justice as compared to self-referred batterers. Their study showed that 66% of the court-referred batterers showed ASPD while 54% of the self-referred showed ASPD. In addition, 66% of the court-referred batterers also met the criteria for Aggressive-Sadistic Personality Disorder as compared to 78% of the self-referred. Babcock, *et al.* (2005) found that ASPD was highly related to violent battering behavior and that autonomic responses (measured by psychophysiological measures) could predict severe battering. Another study (Peek-Asa, *et al.,* 2005) found that batterers tend to be alcohol abusers, have antisocial traits, and constant financial stress. That study found that 13.6 percent of men have performed at least one act of physical abuse. The relationship between alcohol use and battering was studied by Fals-Stewart, *et al.* (2005). They found that men not diagnosed with ASPD are more likely to engage in severe battering when using alcohol. Male ASPDs who abused females appeared to engage in abuse whether or not drinking was present.

Many traditional treatments have completely failed to impact battering and little outcome research has been generated on the newer power and control models. However, MacKenzie (2005) reports that the feminist programs do not significantly reduce recidivism by batterers, but that the newer cognitive-behavioral programs do. In 1995 the authors (Little & Robinson, 1995) modified the MRT® model for use on batterers since research showed that a majority of batterers who are forced into treatment have ASPD. Data from a large Montana implementation of MRT with domestic violence perpetrators (Leonardson, 2000) showed that 41% of all participants showed a prior chemical dependency diagnosis with an additional 9% having another mental health diagnosis. Other client data indicated that over 80% had prior misdemeanor arrests; 43% showed prior felony arrests; and 44% were repeat batterers. Recidivism results from the program showed that only 7.8 percent of MRT completers showed rearrests for battering after one-year, while 13.3 percent of those who did not complete MRT had arrests. Nontreated controls showed a 19 percent one-year rearrest rate for battering. After two-years, the MRT completers showed a 10.8 percent rearrest rate for battering with MRT dropouts showing 22.6 percent. By contrast, nontreated controls showed a two-year rearrest rate for battering of 39.1 percent. All results were statistically significant.

Female Offenders

From the chapters on ASPD, it should be recalled that, within the general population, females have a lower incidence of ASPD than males. However, the diagnostic criteria do not differentiate the symptoms by gender. In essence this means that female ASPDs will show the same characteristics as male ASPDs. Keep in mind however, that the incidence of Borderline Personality Disorder tends to be higher in females as opposed to males.

General cognitive-behavioral approaches for offenders are appropriate for female offenders; however, there are other gender-specific issues that need to be addressed. These include such issues as parenting, codependency, self-esteem, relapse prevention, and vocational/educational programs. This specialized issue has taken on greater importance since females are increasingly becoming a larger proportion of the offender population. According to the National Institute of Justice (BJS, 2005; Morash, Bynum, & Koos, 1998) females are the fastest growing segment in prison and jail populations and one of every four probationers is female. The FBI (2004) has found that 23.2 percent of all American arrests are of females.

Research on female offenders shows that they have gender-specific needs that distinguish them from male offenders (Austin, Bloom, & Donahue, 1992; NIJ, 1998). Female offenders tend to be young mothers, and separation from their children is a major issue. The majority of female offenders have children under the age of 18. Substance abuse and alcohol abuse are also major issues. Various studies (all self-report studies) indicate that from 33 to 75 percent of female offenders report sexual abuse. Sexual abuse, especially childhood sexual abuse, is an area in which few counselors and correctional staff are competent to treat. This issue is more of a mental health concern and specialized services are recommended. "Significant numbers of female offenders are also poorly educated, with unstable employment records. Nearly one-third of the women in the ACA [American Correctional Association] survey never completed high school, and 39 percent quit because they were pregnant ... Many are homeless, drug dependent, and suffer from a variety of health problems including tuberculosis, hepatitis, sexually transmitted diseases, and AIDS. Many are pregnant at at-risk for delivery problems due to poor health, drug abuse, and limited prenatal care" (Austin, Bloom, & Donahue, 1992).

A National Institute of Justice publication (Morash, Bynum, & Koos, 1998) on specific programming needs for female offenders cites the need for a different management style when dealing with female offenders in correctional programs. The report cites that women are more concerned with interpersonal relationships and that they express emotions differently than men. It is recommended that management must effectively respond to expressions of emotions in a way that shows a willingness to communicate openly. A less authoritative style of management is needed. This style includes active listening, patience in explaining rules and program expectations, and staff behaviors that are firm, fair, and consistent. Among the recommendations for effective programs are a multifaceted focus that addresses basic needs and a continuum of care. Participant involvement in the program's operation is also highly desirable. Programs should have clear and measurable goals and be intense and of sufficient duration. Specific programmatic elements that are required are the acquisition of marketable job skills, parenting skills, methods that change faulty thinking and reasoning, and anger management. In addition, specific program elements that deal with victim's issues are necessary including self-esteem, domestic violence, codependency, and self-sufficiency.

In recent years corrections has seen a trend in providing specialized therapeutic communities (TCs) for females within institutions. It is a movement that is to be encouraged. TCs are uniquely able to provide the wide-range of programmatic elements necessary to fully address the many needs seen in this specialized population. The present authors have operated such TCs in several prisons with Moral Reconation Therapy (MRT) serving as the primary treatment. MRT serves to address substance abuse and alcohol issues, relationship issues, and directly confront beliefs, thinking, and reasoning that is asso-

Problems reported by males & females in treatment.
Source: *NIDA Notes*, 20, 2006.

MEN, WOMEN EXPERIENCE DIFFERENT PROBLEMS Women beginning treatment for methamphetamine abuse reported more psychosocial problems, while men reported more crime and criminal justice involvement.

Family and Social Circumstances	Women, % (n=567)	Men, % (n=506)	Total, % (N=1,073)
Children living with someone else by court order	29.3	9.9	20.1
Parental rights terminated	10.1	2.2	6.3
Family abused substances	21.7	10.5	16.4
Physically abused (past month)	5.5	1.8	3.7
Sexually abused (past month)	2.5	0.6	1.6
Employed	23.8	43.9	33.3
On public assistance	63.1	37.0	50.8
Criminal Justice System Involvement			
On parole	4.4	12.7	8.3
On probation	32.3	37.6	34.8
Ever arrested	76.7	88.3	82.2
Arrest in past year	36.7	45.1	40.6
Criminal activity (past month)	55.2	71.7	63.0
Psychiatric Symptoms (Past Month)			
Serious depression	38.8	29.8	34.6
Difficulties with understanding, concentrating, remembering	36.2	26.5	31.6
Suicidal thoughts	11.3	6.3	9.0
Prescribed psychiatric medicine	21.3	15.4	18.6

ciated with criminality and helplessness. These TC units housed 30 to 64 offenders in a closed environment with treatment activities as the continual focus. They are designed to last for a year or more depending on need. A battery of tests were implemented as pre- and post-tests to assess all of the issues relevant to female offenders. The tests included the *Locus of Control* (a measure of self-control), the *Life Purpose Questionnaire* (a measure of perceived purpose in life), the *Sensation Seeking Scale* (a measure of risk-taking), the *Multidimensional Scale of Perceived Social Support* (the degree to which the participant perceives social support from family, friends, and others), and the *Defining Issues Test* (a measure of moral reasoning). Results from over 1,000 program participants have consistently shown desirable and beneficial changes from pre- to posttests (Burnette, *et al.*, 2003; 2005). In addition, recidivism results showed that program participants had significantly lower recidivism as compared to nontreated controls.

Other MRT-based programming (all cognitive-behavioral) was provided to the female TC participants including parenting (Little & Robinson, 1995); relapse prevention (Little, 1997), anger management (Little & Robinson, 1997), codependency (Little & Robinson, 1999), job readiness (Little & Robinson, 1994), and other gender-specific programming focusing on health and educational needs.

Two doctoral dissertations have been conducted on the effectiveness of MRT on female offenders. Pettit (2006) looked at possible differences between 100 incarcerated male and female felons participating in MRT. The study evaluated Readiness to Change scores and locus of control. Readiness to Change is one of the fundamental underpinnings of the Motivational Interviewing method. The study revealed that both males and females participating in MRT showed identical Readiness to Change scores indicating that as participants progressed in MRT, their motivation increased and their level of perceived change increased. Locus of control scores (measuring the degree to which individuals believe they control their lives) showed the same results. Both males and females in MRT showed progressively increased internal control. The study concluded that MRT was an effective treatment approach for female offenders as well as for males.

Schlarb (2009) hypothesized that 156 MRT-treated male and female parolees would show differences in potential recidivism as measured by the Level of Service Inventory-Revised and actual recidivism. While both groups would show some recidivism reduction, Schlarb proposed that based on "Gender Theory" (that females require a specialized gender approach), females would not show the same degree of recidivism reduction as would males. Results of the analysis showed that both males and females showed significant recidivism reductions and that males and females showed nearly identical results.

Mental Health Issues

Mental health is one of the most complex and critical issues in corrections (NIC, 2001; Robison, 2005). Offenders with diagnosable mental disorders such as schizophrenia, mental retardation, Bipolar-Affective Disorder (commonly called manic-depression), depression, and suicidal behavior pose a threat to the order and management of institutions as well as to community supervision programs. Offenders with mental disorders can be a disruptive influence that some staff neither understand nor know how to manage. While the issue of whether individuals who have such diagnosable mental disorders should be placed into the criminal justice system is beyond the scope of this book, the reality is that a relatively small but highly noticeable proportion of offenders (16-25 percent) do have such diagnoses (Robison, 2005). One reality that is often overlooked is when people argue that some disorders, such as mental retardation, cause criminal behaviors. In truth, the vast majority of people with mental disabilities are law abiding and nonviolent. However, just as ASPD can be a co-occurring disorder with the intellectually gifted, it can also be present with mental retardation.

There are many excellent examples of prisons and jails that have established specialized mental health units where offenders with mental disorders are housed and managed. Such programs operate in ways similar to TCs, but ensure that participants receive specialized care and medication to stabilize the disorder. Such units can provide a sense of security to the participants and to other offenders by reducing disruptions and problem situations. Jails, for example, can house a significant number of offenders who are going to go through alcohol withdrawal, which can create not just a life-threatening time period for the specific offender, but also a potentially disruptive and violent course of events due to lack of understanding and inadequate treatment.

Correctional agencies must ensure that the mentally ill offenders under their supervision receive the appropriate medications; thus, identification of such offenders is necessary through screening assessments. This means that intake staff must be trained to identify such needs. In general, the recommendations for mental health offenders include the following: adequate assessment, medication, counseling, separate housing, specialized programs, and regular reviews of status and treatment plans. Specialized staff, links to outside agencies, and a re-entry plan are all necessary (Robison, 2005).

Summary

Robert Hare's (1993) text on ASPDs, *Without Conscience,* captures the essential problems with treating ASPDs. ***ASPD clients simply do not believe that they have a problem and see no reason to change.*** "They never look back with regret or forward with concern. They perceive themselves as superior beings in a dog-eat-dog world in which others are competitors for limited power and resources" (p. 195). Hare goes on to say why many treatments may actually make ASPDs worse. Hare tells us that many inappropriate programs and interventions inadvertently provide the ASPD with excuses and a better way of manipulating and conning others for their personal gain. Programs treating ASPD clients should be cautious in not providing them with any excuses whether it be chemical dependency, abused childhoods, inability to read and write, or inability to get a good, high-paying job. The focus must be taken from *their feelings* and wishes to *their behavior and the effects of their behavior on others.* Perhaps this is why the only effective treatments for the antisocial personality to date are cognitive-behavioral, behavioral, or specific cognitive skills interventions. Such programs avoid discussing client feelings, trying to raise the self-esteem of people who already have inflated esteem, or identifying some cause in their childhood showing how the client is not responsible for their behavior. Slowly, treatment providers are converging on focused treatment techniques that address these concerns. Finally, since research has shown us that we can reduce expected failures (as measured by recidivism) through cognitive-behavioral and purely behavioristic methods, we need to acknowledge that some treatment does beneficially impact the ASPD.

References

ADAM (2008) *ADAM II 2007 Annual Report: Arrestee drug abuse monitoring program II.* Washington DC: Office of Drug Control Policy.

Adamson, S. J., & Sellman, J. D. (2008) Five-year outcomes of alcohol-dependent persons treated with motivational enhancement. *Journal of Studies of Alcohol and Drugs,* 69, 589-593.

American Correctional Association (1990) *The female offender: what does the future hold?* Washington DC: St. Mary's Press.

American Psychiatric Association (2008) *Diagnostic and statistical manual of mental disorders, Fourth Edition, Text Revision.* Arlington, VA: APA.

Anderson, D. A. (1999) The aggregate burden of crime. *Journal of Law and Economics,* October.

Austin, J., Bloom, B., & Donahue, T. (1992) *Female offenders in the community: an analysis of innovative strategies and programs.* San Francisco: National Council on Crime and Delinquency.

Austin, J., Coleman, D., Peyton, J., & Johnson, K. D. (2003) *Reliability and validity study of the LSI-R risk assessment instrument.* Washington, D.C.: The Institute on Crime, Justice and Corrections at the George Washington Univ.; for the Pennsylvania Board of Probation and Parole.

Babcock, J. C., Green, C. E., Webb, S. A., & Yerington, T. P. (2005) Psychophysiological profiles of batterers: autonomic emotional reactivity as it predicts the antisocial spectrum of behavior among intimate partner abusers. *Journal of Abnormal Psychology,* 114, 444-455.

Barkataki, I, Kumari, V., Das, M., Taylor, P., & Sharma, T. (2006) Volumetric structural brain abnormalities in men with schizophrenia or antisocial personality disorder. *Behavioral Brain Research,* 169, 239-247.

Benning, S. D., Patrick, C. J., & Iacono, W. G. (2005) Psychopathy, startle blink modulation, and electrodermal reactivity in twin men. *Psychophysiology,* 42, 753-762.

Birbaumer, N., Veit, R., Lotze, M., Erb, M., Grodd, W., & Flor, H. (2005) Deficient fear conditioning in psychopathy: a functional magnetic resonance imaging study. *Archives of General Psychiatry*, 62, 799-805.

Blair, R. J. (2004) The roles of orbital frontal cortex in the modulation of antisocial behavior. *Brain & Cognition*, 55, 198-208.

Bootzin, R. R., & Acocella, J. R. (1984) *Abnormal psychology: current perspectives*. New York: Random House.

Brennan, T., Dieterich, W., & Ehret, B. (2009) Evaluating the predictive validity of the Compas risk and needs assessment system. *Criminal Justice and Behavior*, 36 (1), 21-40.

Brooner, R. K., Schmidt, C. W., Felch, L. J., & Bigelow, G. E. (1992) Antisocial behavior of intravenous drug abusers: implications for diagnosis of antisocial personality disorder. *American Journal of Psychiatry*, 149, 482-487.

Broughton, L. (2004) Job-Skills program at Tidewater Community College graduates 600 people, shows 95% job placement: Our secret is MRT. *Tidewater Community College Chronicle*, June 17.

Bureau of Justice Statistics (2009) *Correctional Populations*. Washington, DC: U. S. Department of Justice.

Bureau of Justice Statistics (2007) Criminal offenders statistics. Washington DC: U. S. Department of Justice.

Bureau of Justice Statistics (1992a) *Drugs and crime facts:1992*. Washington, DC: U.S. Department of Justice.

Bureau of Justice Statistics (1992b) *Drugs, crime, and the justice system*. Washington, DC: U. S. Department of Justice.

Bureau of Justice Statistics (2008) *Jail Inmates at Midyear-2008*. Washington, DC: U. S. Department of Justice.

Bureau of Justice Statistics (2009) *Key Facts at a Glance*. Washington, DC: U. S. Department of Justice. (http://www.ojp.usdoj.gov/bjs/glance/tables/corr2tab.htm).

Bureau of Justice Statistics (2007; 2005; 1997) *Prison and jail inmates at midyear*. Washington, DC: U. S. Department of Justice.

Bureau of Justice Statistics (2003) *Reentry trends in the United States.* Washington, DC: U. S. Department of Justice.

Burnette, K. D., Brown, P. S., Jackson, K., Thomas-Ottino, B. N., Robinson, K. D., & Little, G. L. (2003) Effects of Moral Reconation Therapy upon female offenders in a prison-based therapeutic community. *Cognitive-Behavioral Treatment Review*, 12, (1) 1-4.

Burnette, K. D., Prachniak, K. J., Leonard, A., Robinson, K. D., Swan, E. S., & Little, G. L. (2005) Effects of Moral Reconation Therapy on female felony offenders in a prison-based therapeutic community. *Cognitive-Behavioral Treatment Review*, 14, (3) 1-4.

Burnette, K. D., Swan, E. S., Robinson, K. D., Woods-Robinson, M., & Little, G. L. (2004) Treating youthful offenders with Moral Reconation Therapy: a recidivism and post-test analysis. *Cognitive-Behavioral Treatment Review*, 13, (3/4) 14-15.

Bursten, B. (1972) The manipulative personality. *Archives of General Psychiatry*, 26, 318-321.

Bush, J. B., Glick, &. Taymans, J. (1997) *Thinking for a Change: Integrated cognitive behavior change program.* Washington, DC: National Institute of Corrections.

Button, T. M., Scourfield, J., Martin, N., Purcell, S., & McGuffin, P. (2005) Family dysfunction interacts with genes in the causation of antisocial symptoms. *Behavioral Genetics*, 35, 115-120.

Chapman, A. H. (1967) *Textbook of clinical psychiatry.* New York: Lippincott.

Cleckley, H. (1964) The *mask of sanity.* St Louis: Mosby.

Colorado Division of Criminal Justice (2007) *Evidence-based correctional practices.* Boulder: Office of Research and Statistics.

Corsini, R. (Ed.) (1973) *Current psychotherapies.* Itasca, IL: Peacock Pubs.

Craig, I. W. (2005) The role of monoamine oxidase A, MAOA, in the aetiology of antisocial behaviours: the importance of gene-environment interactions. *Novartis Foundation Symposium*, 268, 227-237.

Craig, R. J. (1988) A psychometric study of the prevalence of DSM-III Personality Disorders among treated opiate addicts. *The International Journal of the Addictions,* 23, 115-124.

Craig, R. J. (1993) Contemporary trends in substance abuse. *Professional Psychology: Research & Practice,* 24, 182-189.

Davidson, G. M. (1956) The syndrome of oligothymia psychopathy. *Journal of Nervous & Mental Disorders,* 124, 156-162.

Douglas, K. S., Strand, S., Belfrage, H., Fransson, G., & Levander, S. (2005) Reliability and validity evaluation of the Psychopathy Checklist: Screening Version (PCL:SV) in Swedish correctional and forensic psychiatric samples. *Assessment,* 12, 145-161.

Dutton, & Starzomski (1994) Psychological differences between court-referred and self-referred wife assaulters. *Criminal Justice and Behavior,* 21, 203-222.

Eliany, M., & Rush, B. *(1992) How effective are alcohol and other drug prevention and treatment programs?* Canada: Health and Welfare Canada.

Falshow, L., Friendship, C., Travers, R., & Nugent, F. (2004) Searching for 'what works': HM Prison Service accredited cognitive skills programmes. *The British Journal of Forensic Practice,* 6 (2) 3-6.

Fals-Stewart, W., Leonard, K. E., & Birchler, G. R. (2005) The occurrence of male-to-female intimate partner violence on days of men's drinking: the moderating effects of antisocial personality disorder. *Journal of Consulting and Clinical Psychology,* 73, 239-248.

Farabee, D., Nelson, R., & Spence, R. (1993) Psychosocial profiles of criminal justice- and noncriminal justice-referred substance abusers in treatment. *Criminal Justice and Behavior,* 20, 336-346.

FBI (2004) *Crime in the United States, 2004.* Washington DC: FBI.

Fishbein, D. H.(Ed.) (2004) *The science, treatment, and prevention of antisocial behaviors—Volume 1 & 2.* Kingston, NJ: Civic Research Institute.

Flores, A. W., Lowenkamp, C. T., Smith, P., & Latessa, E. J. (2006) Validating the Level of Service Inventory—Revised on a sample of Federal probationers. *Federal Probation,* 70 (2), 1-7.

Foon, A. E. *(1988)* The effectiveness of drinking-driving treatment programs: a critical review. *The International Journal of the Addictions,* 23, 151-174.

Freedman, A. M., Kaplan, H. I., & Saddock, B. J. *(1976) Comprehensive textbook of psychiatry.* Baltimore: Williams & Wilkins.

Freedman, D. (2001) False prediction of future dangerousness: error rates and Psychopathy Checklist-Revised. *Journal of the American Academy of Psychiatry and Law*, 29, 89-95.

Freedman, D. (2001) Premature reliance on the Psychopathy Checklist-Revised in violence risk and threat assessment. *Journal of Threat Assessment*, 1, 51-64.

Freucht, T. E., Stephens, R. C., & Walker, M. L. (1994) Drug use among juvenile arrestees: a comparison of self-report, urinalysis, and hair assay. *The Journal of Drug Issues*, 24, 99-116.

Fridell, M., & Hesse, M. (2006) Psychiatric severity and mortality in substance abusers: a 15-year follow-up of drug users. *Addictive Behaviors*, 31, 559-565.

Fung, M. T., Raine, A., Loeber, R., Lynam, D. R., Steinhauer, S. R., Venables, P. H., & Stouthamer-Lober, M. (2005) Reduced electrodermal activity in psychopathy-prone adolescents. *Journal of Abnormal Psychology*, 114, 187-196.

Gendreau, P., & Ross, R. R. *(1987)* Revivification of rehabilitation: evidence from the *1980s. Justice Quarterly,* 3, 349-407.

Gibbons, D. C. *(1970) Delinquent behavior.* Englewood Cliffs, NJ: Prentice-Hall.

Gilliland, B. E., James, R. K., & Bowman, J. T. *(1994) Theories and strategies in counseling and psychotherapy.* Boston: Allyn and Bacon.

Glaze, L. E., & Palla, S. (2005) Probation and parole in the United States, 2004. Washington DC: Bureau of Justice Statistics.

Goethals, I., Audenaert, K., Jacobs, F., Van den Eynde, F., Bernagie, K., Kolindou, A., Vervaet, M., Dierckx, R., & Van Heeringen, C. (2005) Brain perfusion SPECT in impulsivity-related personality disorders. *Behavioral Brain Research*, 157, 187-192.

Golden, L. (2002) Evaluation of the efficacy of a cognitive behavioral program for offenders on probation: Thinking for a Change. Doctoral dissertation, University of Texas Southwestern Medical Center at Dallas.

Gorski, T. T. *(1993) The chemically dependent criminal offender: recovery and relapse prevention in the criminal justice system.* Independence, MO: Herald House.

Grant, B. F., Hasin, D. S., Stinson, F. S., Dawson, D. A., Chou, S. P., Ruan, W. J., & Pickering, R. P. (2004) Prevalence, correlates, and disability of personality disorders in the United States: Results from the National Epidemiologic Survey on alcohol and other conditions. *Journal of Clinical Psychiatry*, 65, 948-958.

Gunderson, J. (1983) DSM-III diagnosis of personality disorders. In J. Frosch (Ed.) *Current perspectives on personality disorders* (pp. 20-39). Washington, DC:, American Psychiatric Press.

Guze, S. B., & Goodwin, D. W., & Crane, J. B. (1969) Criminality and psychiatric disorders. *Archives of General Psychiatry,* 205, 583-591.

Hardin, C., & Kushner, J. N. (2008) *Quality improvement for drug courts: evidence-based practices.* Alexandria, VA: National Drug Court Institute.

Hare, R. D. (1980) A research scale for the assessment of psychopathy in criminal populations. *Personality and Individual Differences,* 1, 111-117.

Hare, R. D. (1996) Psychopathy and antisocial personality disorder: a case of diagnostic confusion. *Psychiatric Times*, 13.

Hare, R. D. (1993) *Without conscience: the disturbing world of psychopaths among us.* NY: Pocket Books.

Hare, R. D., Hart, S. D., & Harpur, T. J. (1991) Psychopathy and the DSM-IV criteria for Antisocial Personality Disorder. *Journal of Abnormal Psychology,* 100, 391-398.

Hart, S. D., Dutton, & Newlove (1993) The prevalence of personality disorders among wife assaulters. *Journal of Personality Disorders,* 7, 329-341.

Hemphill, J. F., Hart, S. D., & Hare, R. D. (1994) Psychopathy and substance use. *Journal of Personality Disorders,* 8, 169-180.

Hesselbrock, M. N., Meyer, R. E., & Keener, J. J. (1985) Psychopathology in hospitalized alcoholics. *Archives of General Psychiatry,* 42, 1050-1055.

Hilsenroth, M. J., Hibbard, S. R., Nash, M. R., & Handler, L. (1993) A Rorschach study of narcissism, defense, and aggression in Borderline, Narcissistic, and Cluster C Personality Disorders. *Journal of Personality Assessment,* 60, 346-361.

Hindman, J. (1988) New insight into adult and juvenile sexual offenders. *Community Safety Quarterly*, 1, 3.

Hoover Institution (2008) Facts on Policy: Incarceration Rate. March 4, 2008. http://www.hoover.org

Hora, P. F., & Stalcup, T. (2008) Drug treatment courts in the Twenty-First Century: The evolution of the revolution in problem-solving courts. *Georgia Law Review*, 42 (3), 717-811.

Huddleston, C. W., Marlowe, D. B., & Casebolt, R. (2008) *Painting the current picture: a national report card on drug courts and other problem-solving court programs in the United States.* Alexandria, VA: National Drug Court Institute.

Husband, S. D., & Platt, J. J. (1993) The cognitive skills component in substance abuse treatment in correctional settings: a brief review. *Journal of Drug Issues*, 42, 31-41.

Indiana Department of Correction (2008) Juvenile recidivism: 2008. www.in.gov/idoc/files/2008.JuvRecidivismRpt.pdf

Insel, T. R., & Fenton, W. S. (2005) Psychiatric epidemiology: it's not just about counting anymore. *Archives of General Psychiatry*, 62, 590-592.

Jones, M. (1995) Predictors of success and failure of intensive probation supervision. *American Journal of Criminal Justice*, 19, 239-255.

Jovanovic, M. D., Svrakic, D., & Tosevski, D. L. (1993) Personality disorders: a model for conceptual approach and classification. *American Journal of Psychotherapy*, 47, 558-571.

Kappeler, V. E., Blumberg, M., & Potter, G. W. (2000) *The mythology of crime and criminal justice.* Prospect Heights, IL: Waveland.

Kessler, R. C., Berglund, P., & Demler, et al. (2005) Lifetime prevalence and age-of-onset distributions in DSM-IV disorders in the National Comorbidity Survey replication. *Archives of General Psychiatry*, 62, 593-602.

Kessler, R. C., Chiu, W. T., Demler, O., & Walters, E. E. (2005) Prevalence, severity, and comorbidity of 12-month DSM-IV disorders in the National Comorbidity Survey replication. *Archives of General Psychiatry*, 62, 617-627.

Kessler, R. C., McGonagle, K. A., Zhao, S., Nelson, C. B., Hughes, M., Eshleman, S., Wittchen, H., & Kendler, K. S. (1994) Lifetime and 12-month prevalence of DSM-III-R psychiatric disorders in the United States. *Archives of General Psychiatry,* 51, 8-19.

Kirchner, R. A. & Goodman, E. (2007) Effectiveness and impact of Thurston County, Washington drug court program. *Cognitive-Behavioral Treatment Review,* 16 (2), 1-4.

Kirchner, R. A. & Kirchner, T. (2008) Improving Putnam County, Florida criminal justice system: effectiveness of drug treatment court. *Cognitive-Behavioral Treatment Review,* 17 (2), 1-3.

Khantzian, E. J., & Treece, C. (1985) DSM-III psychiatric diagnosis of narcotic addicts. *Archives of General Psychiatry, 442,* 1067-1071.

Kleinman, P. H., Miller, A. B., Millman, R. B., Woody, G. E., Todd, T., Kemp, J., & Lipton, D. S. (1990) Psychopathology among cocaine abusers entering treatment. *Journal of Nervous and Mental Disease,* 178, 442-447.

Kolb, L. C. *(1968) Noyes' modern clinical psychiatry.* Philadelphia: W. B.. Saunders.

Kroner, D. G., Mills, J. F., & Reddon, J. R. (2005) A coffee can, factor analysis, and prediction of antisocial behavior: the structure of criminal risk. *International Journal of Law & Psychiatry,* 28, 360-374.

Lawson, G. W., Ellis, D. C., & Rivers, P. C. *(1984) Essentials of chemical dependency counseling.* Rockville, MD: Aspen Publishers.

Leiber, M. J., & Mawhorr, T. L. (1995) Evaluating the use of cognitive skills training and employment with delinquent youth. *Journal of Criminal Justice,* 23,127-141.

Leonardson, G. R. (2000) Montana-based program shows reductions in domestic violence rearrests after treatment. *Cognitive-Behavioral Treatment Review,* 9 (1), 1-3.

Leukefeld, C. G., & Tims, F. M. (1992*) Drug abuse treatment in prisons and jails.* Rockville, MD: NIDA.

Lipton, D. S., Falkin, G. P., & Wexler, H. A. (1990) *Correctional drug abuse treatment in the United States: an overview.* Rockville, MD: NIDA.

Little, G. L. (2000-2002) Cognitive-behavioral treatment of offenders: a comprehensive review of MRT outcome research. *Addictive Behaviors Treatment Review,* 2 (1), 12-21.

Little, G. L. (1992) *Cognitive behavioral treatments applied to substance abusers: a monograph.* Memphis, TN: Eagle Wing Books, Inc.

Little, G. L. (2006) Meta-analysis of Moral Reconation Therapy recidivism results from probation and parole implementations. *Cognitive-Behavioral Treatment Review*, 14 (1-2), 14-16.

Little, G. L. (2006) MRT in drug courts: a comprehensive review of recidivism outcomes. *Cognitive-Behavioral Treatment Review*, 15 (2), 1-6.

Little, G. L. (1997) *Psychopharmacology: Basics For Counselors.* Memphis: Advanced Training Associates.

Little, G. L. (2006) Recidivism outcome research on Moral Reconation Therapy in prison-based therapeutic communities: a comprehensive review. *Cognitive-Behavioral Treatment Review*, 15 (2), 14-17.

Little, G. L. (1997) *Staying Quit: A Cognitive-Behavioral Workbook for Relapse Prevention.* Memphis: Advanced Training Associates.

Little, G. L. (1996) Relapse Prevention: an overview. *Focus, 2.*

Little, G. L., & Robinson, K. D. (1995) *Bringing peace to relationships: an MRT® educational workbook.* Memphis: Eagle Wing Books, Inc.

Little, G. L., & Robinson, K. D. (1997) *Coping with anger: a cognitive-behavioral workbook.* Memphis: Eagle Wing Books, Inc.

Little, G., & Robinson, K. D. (1994) Cost effectiveness, rehabilitation potential, and safety of intermediate sanctions: mixed results. *Cognitive-Behavioral Treatment Review,* 3 (1), 4-7.

Little, G. L., & Robinson, K. D. (1989) Effects of Moral Reconation Therapy on moral reasoning, life purpose, and recidivism among drug and alcohol offenders. *Psychological Reports,* 64, 83-90.

Little, G. L., & Robinson, K. D. (1988) *How to escape your prison.* Memphis TN: Eagle Wing Books, Inc.

Little, G. L., & Robinson, K. D. (1994) *Job Readiness.* Memphis TN: Eagle Wing Books, Inc.

Little, G. L., & Robinson, K. D. (1988) Moral Reconation Therapy: a systematic step-by-step treatment system for treatment resistant clients. *Psychological Reports,* 62, 135-151.

Little, G. L., & Robinson, K. D. (1995) *Parenting and family values: an MRT® educational workbook.* Memphis: Eagle Wing Books, Inc.

Little, G., & Robinson, K. D. (2006) Recidivism outcome research on Moral Reconation Therapy in prison-based therapeutic communities: a comprehensive review. *Cognitive-Behavioral Treatment Review,* 15 (2), 14-17.

Little, G. L., & Robinson, K. D. (1990) Reducing recidivism by changing how inmates think: the systematic approach of Moral Reconation Therapy. *American Jails,* 4(3), 12-16.

Little, G. L., & Robinson, K. D. (1989) Relationship of DUI recidivism to moral reasoning, sensation seeking, and MacAndrew alcoholism scores. *Psychological Reports,* 65, 1171-1174.

Little, G. L., & Robinson, K. D. (1989) Treating drunk drivers with Moral Reconation Therapy: a one-year recidivism report. *Psychological Reports,* 64, 960-962.

Little, G. L., & Robinson, K. D. (1990) Treating drunk drivers with Moral Reconation Therapy: a two-year recidivism report. *Psychological Reports,* 66, 1379-1387.

Little, G. L., & Robinson, K. D. (1997) *Understanding and treating Antisocial Personality Disorder.* Memphis: Eagle Wing Books, Inc.

Little, G. L., & Robinson, K. D. (1999) *Untangling relationships: dealing with codependency using the MRT model.* Memphis: Eagle Wing Books, Inc.

Little, G. L., Robinson, K. D., & Burnette, K. D. (1992) Cognitive-behavioral treatment for offenders. The *IARCA Journal on Community Corrections,* September, 5-9.

Little, G. L., Robinson, K. D., & Burnette, K. D. (1993) Cognitive behavioral treatment of felony drug offenders: a five-year recidivism report. *Psychological Reports,* 73, 1089-1090.

Little, G. L., Robinson, K. D., & Burnette, K. D. (1991) Treating drug offenders with Moral Reconation Therapy: a three-year recidivism report. *Psychological Reports,* 69, 1151-1154.

Little, G. L., Robinson, K. D., & Burnette, K. D. (1991) Treating drunk drivers with Moral Reconation Therapy: a three-year recidivism report. *Psychological Reports,* 69, 953-954.

Little, G. L., Robinson, K. D., Burnette, K. B., & Swan, E. S. (1996) Review of outcome data with MRT®: seven year recidivism results. *Cognitive-Behavioral Treatment Review*, 5, (1), 1-7.

Little, G. L., Robinson, K. D., Burnette, K. B., & Swan, E. S. (1999a) Successful ten-year outcome data on MRT-treated felony offenders. *Cognitive-Behavioral Treatment Review*, 8, (1), 1-3.

Little, G. L., Robinson, K. D., Burnette, K. B., & Swan, E. S. (1999) Ten-year outcome data on MRT-treated DWI offenders. *Cognitive-Behavioral Treatment Review*, 8, (2), 1-4.

Little, G. L., Robinson, K. D., Burnette, K. B., & Swan, E. S. (2010) Twenty-year recidivism results on MRT-treated offenders. *Cognitive-Behavioral Treatment Review*, 19, (1), 1-4.

Lowenkamp, C.T., & Latessa, E. J. (2006) Evaluation of Thinking for a Change: Tippecanoe County, Indiana. Cincinnati: University of Cincinnati.

Lynam, D. R., Caspi, A., Moffitt, T. E., Raine, A., Lober, R., & Stouthamer-Lober, M. (2005) Adolescent psychopathy and the big five: results from two samples. *Journal of Abnormal Child Psychology*, 33, 431-443.

MacKay, J. R. (1986) Psychopathy and pathological narcissism: a descriptive and psychodynamic formulation on the Antisocial Personality Disorder. *Journal of Offender Counseling, Services & Rehabilitation*, 11, 77-94.

MacKenzie. D. L. (2006) *What works in corrections: reducing the criminal activities of offenders and delinquents*. New York: Cambridge Univ. Press.

Magura, S., Kang, S. Y., & Shapiro, J. L. (1995) Measuring cocaine use by hair analysis among criminally-involved youth. *The Journal of Drug Issues, 25,* 683-701.

Malow, R. M., West, J. A., Williams, J. L., & Sutker, P. B. (1989) Personality Disorders classification and symptoms in cocaine and opioid addicts. *Journal of Consulting and Clinical Psychology, 57,* 765-767.

Martinson, R. (1979) What works? Questions and answers about prison reform. *Public Interest*, 35, 22-54.

Mason, D. A., & Frick, P. J. (1994) The heritability of antisocial behavior: a meta-analysis of twin and adoption studies. *Journal of Psychopathology and Behavioral Assessment*, 16, 301-323.

McCabe, J. (2009) Sustaining the gain: Wellness court alumni group. *Cognitive-Behavioral Treatment Review*, 18 (1/2), 1-3.

McCracken, L. (2003) Juvenile DWI/drug court, Albuquerque, NM. *Cognitive-Behavioral Treatment Review*, 12 (1), 8-9.

Mendez, M. F., Chen, A. K., Shapira, J. S., & Miller, B. L. (2005) Acquired sociopathy and frontotemporal dementia. *Dementia and Geriatric Cognitive Disorders*, 20, 99-104.

Mervis, J. (1986) Rehabilitation: can it work now? APA *Monitor*, September, 14.

Milkman, H., & Wanberg, K. (2007) *Cognitive-behavioral treatment: A review and discussion for corrections professionals*. Washington, DC: National Institute of Corrections.

Morash, M., Bynum, T. S., & Koons, B. A. (1998) *Women offenders: programming needs and promising approaches*. Washington DC: National Institute of Justice.

Morgan, R. L., Eagle, S. G., Esser, E., & Roth, W. M. (1993) Moral reasoning in adjucated youth residing at a boy's ranch. *Journal of Correctional Education*, 44, 62-66.

Myers, D. G. (1992) *Psychology*. New York: Worth.

Narayan, V. M., Narr, K. L., Kumari, V., Woods, R. P., Thompson, P. M., Toga, A. W., & Sharma, T. (2007 Regional cortical thinning in subjects with violent antisocial personality disorder or schizophrenia. *American Journal of Psychiatry*, 164, 1418-1427.

National Institute of Corrections (2004) *Implementing evidence-based practice in community corrections: the principles of effective intervention*. Washington DC: U.S. Department of Justice.

National Institute of Corrections (2001) *Provisions of mental health care in prisons: special issues in corrections*. Washington DC: U.S. Department of Justice.

National Institute of Justice (1995) *Report on the violence against women research strategic planning workshop*. Washington: NIJ.

National Institute on Drug Abuse (2002) *Therapeutic community*. Washington DC: NIDA.

NIDA Notes (2008) New technique links 89 genes to drug dependence. *NIDA Notes*, 22 (1), 6-8.

Norden, K. A., Klein, D. N., Donaldson, S., Pepper, C. N., & Klein, L. M. (1995) Reports of the early home environment in DSM III-R personality disorders. *Journal of Personality Disorders*, 9, 213-223.

O'Boyle, M. (1993) Personality disorder and multiple substance dependence. *Journal of Personality Disorders*, 7, 342-347.

Overholser, W., & Owens, D. J. (1961) The "psychopath": some legal and treatment aspects. *Journal of Social Therapy*, 7, 127-134.

Page, J. D. (1971) *Psychopathology*. Chicago: Aldine - Atherton.

Palmer, T. (1993) *Programmatic and nonprogrammatic aspects of successful intervention*. LaCrosse, WI: IARCA.

Peer-Asa, C., Zwerling, C., Young, T., Stromquist, A. M., Burmeister, L. F., & Merchant, J. A. (2005) A population based study of reporting patterns and characteristics of men who abuse their female partners. *Injury Prevention*, 11, 180-185.

Penick, E., Powell, J. Othmer, E., et al. (1984) Subtyping alcoholics by co-existing psychiatric syndromes. In: *Longitudinal research in alcoholism*. D. W. Goodwin, R. T. Van Dusen, S. A. Mednick (Eds.). Hingham, Mass.: Kluwer-Nijhoff.

Pennington, L. A., & Berg, I. A. (1954) *An introduction to clinical psychology*. New York: Ronald Press.

Petersilia, S. T. (1986) Prison versus probation in California: Implications for crime and offender recidivism. Washington, DC: National Institute of Justice; Rand Co.

Petersilia, J. (2004) What works in prisoner reentry? Reviewing and questioning the evidence. *Federal Probation*, 68 (2): 4–8.

Pettit, J. R. (2006) Readiness to change and locus of control in female offenders. Unpublished dissertation: University of Memphis.

Phelps, L., & McClintock, K. (1994) Papa and peers: a biosocial approach to conduct disorder. *Journal of Psychopathology and Behavioral Assessment*, 16, 53-67.

Pridmore, S., Chambers, A., & McArthur, M. (2005) Neuroimaging in psychopathy. *Australian and New Zealand Journal of Psychiatry*, 39, 856-865.

Pugh, D. N. (1993) The effects of problem-solving ability and locus of control on prisoner adjustment. *International Journal of Offender Therapy and Comparative Criminology*, 163-176.

Ratliff, M. S. (1993) Classification of male substance-abusing incarcerated offenders and treatment indications: a cluster-analytic study. Unpublished dissertation, Nashville: Vanderbilt University.

Reid, W. H. (1985) The antisocial personality: a review. *Hospital and Community Psychiatry*, 36, 831-837.

Resnick, H. S., Foy, D. W., Donahoe, C. P., & Miller, E. N. (1989) Antisocial behavior and Post-Traumatic Stress Disorder in Vietnam veterans. *Journal of Clinical Psychology*, 45, 860-866.

Robins, L. N. (1966) *Deviant children grown up: a sociological and psychiatric study of sociopathic personality.* Baltimore: Williams & Wilkins.

Robins, L., & Regier, D. (Eds.). (1991) *Psychiatric disorders in America.* New York: Free Press.

Robinson, K. D., & Little, G. L. (1989) Drugs and criminal justice issues. In A. J. Giannini & A. E. Slaby (Eds.), *Drugs of abuse.* Oradell, NJ: Medical Economics Books. Pp. 427-440.

Robinson, K. D., & Little, G. L. (1987) One-day dropouts from correctional drug treatment. *Psychological Reports*, 51, 409-410.

Robison, C. (2005) National overview of mental health issues in corrections. Columbus, OH: Correctional Institution Inspection Committee.

Rosenthal, D. (1970) *Genetic theory and abnormal behavior.* New York: McGraw Hill.

Ross, R.R & Fabiano, E. A. (1985) *Time to think: A cognitive model of delinquency prevention and offender rehabilitation.* Johnson City, TN: Institute of Social Sciences and Arts, Inc.

Rounsaville, B. J., & Kleber, H. D. (1985) Untreated opiate addicts: how do they differ from those seeking treatment? *Archives of General Psychiatry*, 42, 1072-1077.

Samenow, S. E. (1984) *Inside the criminal mind.* New York: Times Books.

Schlarb, A. M. (2009) A comparison of the effects of a cognitive behavioral program between male and female parolees. Unpublished dissertation, Walden University.

Shea, M. T., Widiger, T. A., & Klein, M. H. (1992) Comorbidity of Personality Disorders and Depression: implications for treatment. *Journal of Consulting and Clinical Psychology,* 60, 857-868.

Sherman, L. W. (1993) Defiance, deterrence, and irrelevance: a theory of the criminal sanction. *Journal of Research in Crime & Delinquency,* 30, 445-473.

Sherman, L. W., Farrington, D. P., Welsh, B. C., & MacKenzie, D. L. (2002) *Evidence-based crime prevention.* NY: Routledge.

Sickmund, M. (2009) Delinquency cases in juvenile court, 2005. Washington DC: OJJDP.

Skeem, J. L., Edens, J. F., Camp, J., & Colwell, L. H. (2004) Are there ethnic differences in levels of psychopathy: a meta-analysis. *Law and Human Behavior,* 28, 505-527.

Smith, C., & Thornberry, T. P. (1995) The relationship between childhood maltreatment and adolescent involvement in delinquency. *Criminology,* 33, 451-477.

Snyder, H. N., & Sickmund, M. (1995) *Juvenile offenders and victims: a national report.* Pittsburgh: National Center for Juvenile Justice.

Solomon, A. L. (2006) Does parole supervision work? Research findings and policy opportunities. *Perspectives,* Spring, 26-37.

Spiecker, B. (1988) Psychopathy: the incapacity to have moral emotions. *Journal of Moral Education,* 17, 98-104.

State of Washington (2005) Recidivism of juvenile offenders. Olympia, WA: Sentencing Guidelines Commission.

Swan, N. (1993) Researchers probe which comes first: drug abuse or antisocial behavior. *NIDA Notes,* May/June, 6-7.

Sweet. R. S., Little, G. L., Wood, R. W., & Harrison, H. D. (1977) A drug offender rehabilitation program: recovery rates, personality variables, and maintenance factors. *The Quarterly Journal of Corrections,* 1, 13-22.

Tobey, L. H., & Bruhn, A. R. (1992) Early memories and the criminally dangerous. *Journal of Personality Assessment,* 59,137-152.

Tolan, P., & Guerra, N. (1994) *What works in reducing adolescent violence: an empirical review of the field.* Boulder, CO: Center for the Study and Prevention of Violence.

University of Michigan (2008) National Results on Adolescent Drug Use. *News and Information Services.* Dec. 11, 2008.

Van Kamen, W. B., & Loeber, R. (1994) Are fluctuations in delinquent activities related to the onset and offset in juvenile illegal drug use and drug dealing? *The Journal of Drug Issues,* 24, 9-24.

Veneziano, C., & Veneziano, L. (1992) The relationship between deterrence and moral reasoning. *Criminal Justice Review,* 17, 209-217.

Viding, E., Blair, R. J., Moffitt, T. E., & Plomin, R. (2005) Evidence for substantial genetic risk for psychopathy in 7-year-olds. *Journal of Child Psychology and Psychiatry,* 46, 592-597.

Walker, S. (2001) *Sense and nonsense about crime and drugs.* Belmont, CA: Wadsworth.

Walsh, Z., Swogger, M. T., & Kosson, D. S. (2004) Psychopathy, IQ, and violence in European American and African American county jail inmates. *Journal of Consulting and Clinical Psychology,* 72, 1165-1169.

Wanberg, K., &. Milkman, H. (2001) *Criminal Conduct and Substance Abuse Treatment: Strategies for Self-Improvement and Change (SSC); A report on provider training, staff development and client involvement in SSC treatment.* Denver: Center for Interdisciplinary Studies.

Wang, P. S., Lane, M., Olfson, M., et al. (2005) Twelve-month use of mental health services in the United States: results from the National Comorbidity Survey replication. *Archives of General Psychiatry,* 62, 629-640.

Warren, J., Gelb, A., Horowitz, J., & Riordan, J. (2008) *One in 100: Behind bars in America 2008.* Pew Center on the States and the Public Safety Performance Project.

Washington State Institute for Public Policy (2006) *Evidence-based adult corrections programs: what works and what does not.* Olympia, WA.

Widiger, T., Frances, A., Spitzer, R., & Williams, J. (1988) The DSM-III-R personality disorders: an overview. *American Journal of Psychiatry,* 145, 786-795.

Wilkinson, J. (2005) Evaluating evidence for the effectiveness of the Reasoning and Rehabilitation Programme. *Howard Journal of Criminal Justice* 44(1): 70–85.

Wolman, B. B. (Ed.) (1965) *Handbook of clinical psychology.* New York: McGraw Hill.

Wood, R. W., & Sweet, R. S. (1974) Comprehensive report on the drug offender rehabilitation program at the Shelby County Penal Farm, Memphis, TN. LEAA, U. S. Department of Justice.

Woody, G. E., McClellan, T., Luborsky, L., & O'Brien, C. P. (1985) Sociopathy and psychotherapy outcome. *Archives of General Psychiatry,* 42, 1081-1086.

Yang, Y., Raine, A., Lencz, T., Bihrle, S., Lacasse, L., & Colletti, P. (2005) Prefrontal white matter in pathological liars. *British Journal of Psychiatry,* 187, 326-327.

Yang, Y., Raine, A., Lencz, T., Bihrle, S., Lacasse, L., & Colletti, P. (2005) Volume reduction in prefrontal gray matter in unsuccessful criminal psychopaths. *Biological Psychiatry,* 57, 1103-1108.

Zhang, Z. (2003; 2007) *Drug and alcohol use and related matters among arrestees.* Washington, DC: ADAM.

Index

About The Authors

Dr. Gregory L. Little received his Doctor of Education Degree in Counseling and Educational Psychology and a Master of Science Degree in Psychology from the University of Memphis. He is a Nationally Certified Psychologist (NAMP) and a licensed professional counselor and is the co-developer of Moral Reconation Therapy (MRT®). Dr. Little has published several hundred articles in criminal justice, psychology, and substance abuse treatment. He taught at Shelby State Community College and Louisiana State University-Shreveport and served as the Director of Drug & Alcohol Programs for 10 years at the largest correctional institute in Tennessee. He has authored or co-authored over 40 books including a variety of treatment workbooks and textbooks on psychopharmacology, criminal treatment, and counseling. He has been featured in over a dozen documentaries appearing on the *National Geographic Channel, MSNBC, Discovery*, the *History Channel*, the *Learning Channel, BBC, SyFy*, the *Weather Channel*, and *Vision TV*. Dr. Little is part Native American (Seneca) and has written numerous books in archaeology including *The Illustrated Encyclopedia of Native American Mounds and Earthworks*.

Dr. Kenneth D. Robinson received his Doctor of Education Degree in Educational Psychology and Counseling and a Master of Science Degree in Psychology from the University of Memphis. He is President of Correctional Counseling, Inc. and is the co-developer of Moral Reconation Therapy (MRT®), which is listed on SAMHSA's National Registry of Evidence-Based Programs. He is Executive Editor of *Cognitive Behavioral Treatment Review* and was Executive Editor of *ACRIM News* in 1993-1994 and Associate Editor of *Recovery Times* in 1990-1992. He was Director of Clinical Services and Director of the Crisis Stabilization Unit for Midtown Mental Health Center in Memphis, Tennessee. He also worked in Mental Health Services for the Shelby County Correction Center from 1975-1987 and worked for a year with Project CERCE at the State Regional Prison in Memphis. Dr. Robinson conducts frequent training and workshops in MRT throughout the United States, the UK, Australia, and Puerto Rico. He has published and presented hundreds of professional articles in the areas of psychopharmacology, criminal treatment, and mental health. He is co-author of all of the MRT treatment materials and other books including *How To Escape Your Prison, Your Inner Enemy, Filling The Inner Void, Character Development, Family Support, Job*

Readiness, Understanding & Treating The Antisocial Substance Abuser, Parenting and Family Values, Discovering Life & Liberty in the Pursuit of Happiness, Coping With Anger, and *Bringing Peace To Relationships.* Dr. Robinson is also coauthor of numerous textbooks including *Effective Counseling Approaches for Criminal Offenders, Crisis Intervention, Understanding and Treating Antisocial Personality Disorder, The Punishment Myth,* and *Your LifeWork.* In addition, Dr. Robinson has coauthored *The Journey to Freedom, Tools for a Fresh Start, Personal Responsibility Parenting,* and all of the Social Responsibility Training (SRT®) materials. He received a Presidential Citation from the American Psychological Association in May 2009 for Innovative Practice Strategies to Address Social and Behavioral Problems of At-Risk Youth. He is on the faculty of the National Judicial College, National Drug Court Institute, and National DWI Treatment Staff Training for NTSHA.

Katherine Burnette holds a Masters Degree in Psychology from the University of Memphis and is a licensed alcohol and drug abuse counselor. She has been a Vice President of Correctional Counseling, Inc. since 1991. She has published numerous professional articles in the areas of criminal justice and substance abuse along with coauthoring several books including *Effective Counseling Approaches for Criminal Offenders, Crisis Intervention,* and *Your LifeWork.* She is a national trainer for Moral Reconation Therapy® and MRT® for domestic violence treatment. She has been in the criminal justice treatment field for 25 years and has been responsible for implementing, managing, and providing oversight to a variety of state correctional departments and agencies.

E. Stephen Swan holds a Masters Degree in Counseling from the University of Memphis and worked for over 20 years in one of the largest local correctional systems in the United States. He has served as Programs Manager and Correctional Administrator at the largest Tennessee correctional institution (3,500 beds). He has been a Vice President with Correctional Counseling, Inc. since 1994. He is a national Moral Reconation Therapy® trainer, criminal justice consultant, and Editor of *Cognitive-Behavioral Treatment Review.* He has coauthored numerous journal articles on criminal justice treatments and has presented at a host of criminal justice conferences and workshops.